"Our best hope as we navigate the realities of a divided and highly polarized world is to find a love, listen, and collaborate across faith and politics not just despite our differences but because we know we need each other. Amanda Henderson is the perfect voice for these tumultuous times. With on the ground experience and the kind of leadership we desperately need for a better future, she offers us tangible ways to do our own inner work, bridge divides, and embody healthy change our world desperately needs. *Holy Chaos* is the perfect book for individuals and communities who want to not only learn but transform that learning into action." —Kathy Escobar, co-pastor of The Refuge and author of *Practicing: Changing Yourself to Change the World*

"I wish I could go back twenty years in time and give myself a copy of Amanda Henderson's beautiful new book, *Holy Chaos*. It would have saved me so many mistakes. It would have inspired me to take worthwhile risks. It would have comforted me when the work of peace-making and justice-seeking seemed terribly hard. I'm so glad this book is now available for you, because we need you, right now, to become an agent in the holy work of building connections in these divisive times." —Brian D. McLaren, author/speaker/activist

"Amanda Henderson is a wise and generous teacher. She draws from her own experiences as pastor, activist, and (most importantly) family member to show us all that every moment is an opportunity for building relationships. In these fractured times, no one is more cherished than someone who can help us put the pieces back together. I am blessed to know her and learn from her." —Jack Moline, president, Interfaith Alliance

"Gracefully written, this book is a documented guide that leads its readers through a mix of religion and politics, fear and love, diversity and unity, poetry and prose, diversity and cooperation, defeat and joy, surprisingly opening readers' minds to the insightful interaction of what at first glance seem to be contradictions. With unique skill, the author draws from multiple religions not to highlight differences or peddle ideologies but to introduce life-enhancing wisdom helpful for everybody." —C. Welton Gaddy, president emeritus, Interfaith Alliance; pastor emeritus, Northminster Church; host, *State of Belief* radio program

"There are many ways to live our lives; by far the most powerful and dangerous is to live vulnerably. And this is precisely why *Holy Chaos* is both powerful and dangerous. Amanda not only invites us toward vulnerability but makes herself vulnerable on every page of this book. In doing so, she invites us to live this kind of life, and reveals this is fertile soil for us to come together, across our pain and difference, to pursue peace and justice." —Michael Hidalgo, lead pastor, Denver Community Church, author of *Changing Faith: Questions, Doubts and Choices about the Unchanging God*

"If you have ever experienced chaos in your world, community, family, or your own heart, Amanda Henderson's wise book is for you. She offers no easy answers, rather telling stories about her own and others' experiences and inviting reflection on the holiness of our messy lives. *Holy Chaos* is a necessary book for these divisive times." —Jane E. Vennard, spiritual director and author of *Fully Awake and Truly Alive: Spiritual Practices to Nurture Your Soul*

"Amanda Henderson's *Holy Chaos* is a powerful guide for people of faith who are perplexed by the challenges of our age and wondering how we might respond in impactful ways. Drawing on her stories and expertise as a pastor and community organizer, Henderson has written a book chock-full of practical insights and provocative invitations to create holy chaos in our communities to bring about the healing and redemption that our world so desperately longs for. This book is required reading for every community of faith seeking to make an impact in their world!" —Brandan Robertson, lead pastor of Missiongathering Christian Church, San Diego, and author of *True Inclusion: Creating Communities of Radical Embrace*

"Never has the release of a book been so well timed. As people of faith navigate the turbulent waters of our nation's politics, it is helpful to have a guide that can bring us safely into harbor without sacrificing our souls. Amanda Henderson has not only studied the waters, but has braved them herself, leaping head first into the deep end of faith and politics. Whether she is in the capitol in a clergy collar standing against unjust systems or in a T-shirt and jeans passing out PBJ's to our homeless brothers and sisters, Rev. Henderson lives her faith. Read *Holy Chaos*, and you will be better at living yours as well." —Jerry Herships, founder of AfterHours Denver, author of *Last Call and Rogue Saints*

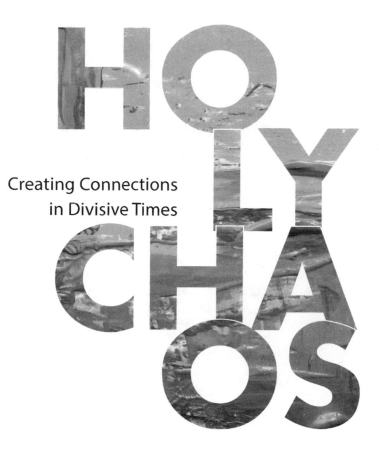

HOLY CHAOS

Creating Connections
in Divisive Times

Amanda Henderson

chalice

ChalicePress.com

Print: 9780827215153

EPUB: 9780827215160

EPDF: 9780827215177

Printed in the United States of America

For Kyle,
Mia, Faith, & Ryan
For our little space in the world
where we learn how to grow,
how to struggle,
how to experience joy and laughter
in the midst of it all
—while loving each other *still*.

Contents

Prelude

In the Midst

The morning after the 2016 presidential election, I sat, like so many others, feeling shock and deep concern for the future of our country and for my children. That same morning my father was scheduled for surgery. I was to meet my parents at the hospital two miles from my house at 8:00 a.m. I knew my parents were happy about the election results; they had the hats to prove it. I was heartbroken. I didn't understand how my mother, a strong independent woman who has always judged a man's character by his marital fidelity and treatment of women (to the point of refusing to watch movies with stars who have mistreated their wives), could vote for a person with such a horrific track record with women. I was baffled that my father, a life-long computer and science guy who values facts, could give a pass to the lies and science denial coming from the new President. Throughout the campaign season, we had spent many hours together in crowded hospital rooms, rotating between uncomfortable chairs and a pull-out bed. We had unfortunately gotten into heated debates about presidential politics, and I was not interested in reliving that tension on this day. On this painful morning I knew I needed to bracket my emotions about the election and focus on caring for my parents by being present and compassionate.

So when I awoke, I rolled over and sent my mother a text message letting her know I was upset about the election, was not ready to talk about it, and instead wanted to focus my energy on Dad's healing. My parents respected my wishes; they, too, felt singularly focused on my Dad's surgery. So, we sat together in the waiting room ignoring the political headlines on the covers of magazines scattered on coffee tables and glancing past the four televisions showing multiple news stations replaying the election results from the previous night. We laughed about how the grandkids had hoped that Papa's surgery could have excused them from school that day, and we called my sister to let her know we would be heading in to see the doctor soon. We made a few jokes about the fact that my dad had had the good luck to be diagnosed with a disease with a name that sounded straight out of *Star Trek*—carcinoid cancer. Two hours later, they wheeled him back; my mom and I waved to him as he went into the surgery room, and we hugged to reassure ourselves that all would be well. It was. He came out of surgery an hour later. Doctors had removed the small tumor, and he would now rest for the evening, a rhythm to which we had unfortunately become accustomed.

Later that night I returned home, still reeling with the emotions of all that was stirring personally and politically. I wondered what the election would mean for the communities I care about personally and the people for whom I advocate daily in my work as Executive Director of the Interfaith Alliance of Colorado.

For the past five years I have been working to bring people together from multiple religious traditions to advocate on the basis of our shared values for human rights and equality. I am an ordained minister and a mom to three teenagers. I have been married for more than twenty years and love our neighborhood and community with all my heart. I experience joy through running, raising animals, growing plants and gardens, and spending time with friends. I love all of the people in my life fiercely. I also spend time each day standing with marginalized communities, bringing people together, and advocating for systemic transformation.

My days are typically filled with meetings: meeting with Muslim communities to counter Islamophobia, getting to know immigrant families who are working to establish community, and ensuring that women's reproductive rights and health are protected. On this particular day I just kept thinking about the many people I love and for whom I care who would be affected by the proposed policies and divisive rhetoric of the new President. I thought of my friend Jeanette, who was already living in a sanctuary to avoid deportation after more than twenty years raising her children in this country. I thought of my friend Paula, who would be vulnerable to discrimination and have less legal protection as a transgender woman. And I thought of my children, who would inherit the long-term consequences of diminished environmental protections and courts stacked with justices who were against many of the concerns of everyday people and especially against women's reproductive freedom.

Yet as I wallowed in grief, I realized I was not alone. This is how most of the world has lived for most of history. Rarely are leaders on the side of the people. Quite often, there are radically different views and experiences within societies and even within individual families. In the United States, people of color, immigrants, Native people, and any other marginalized group have rarely felt safe, seen as valuable by those in power, or free to thrive. And yet, despite the uncertainty and chaos, people build resilience, speak the truth, work for healing, fight for change, and, most importantly, love one another and create space for joy and celebration.

Over the past four years since that 2016 election, the deep wounds in our country, our communities, and even our families have been on full display. Sometimes it seems we are living in different worlds depending on to what news we listen or with what circle of friends we surround ourselves. I feel real concern about the divisiveness in rhetoric, about the policies that marginalize people and tear families apart, and about the realization that the only way through all of this is to stand fiercely for human dignity and to build relationships with people whose views differ substantially from my own.

This is one of the more chaotic and unprecedented times in our US history. When I wrote this book, I imagined the chaotic and unprecedented time would be related to the impending 2020 presidential election. However, we have a turn of events that has created division in ways that are unique to this moment. As I send this book for publishing, we are under a "shelter in place order" to try to stop the *coronavirus pandemic*. As this virus sweeps across the world, we have seen over a million people infected and the global economy come to a halt. At this moment more than 20,000 people have died in the United States, a number that is expected to grow to 100,000 to 200,000 people. While so often our reaction to times of crisis is to *gather*, to hold one another, to share meals and connection, this time the response requires *physical distance*. In order to love our neighbor, we must stay in our own house. In order to care for the most vulnerable among us, we must assure that medical providers have what they need, and the rest of us must simply stay in place to stop the spread. This goes against all of my instincts to run toward the pain, physically.

Unlike pivotal moments of shared pain, such as the attacks of September 11, 2001, or school shootings, or the many wars of our history, this is not a tragedy born out of hate and violence. Unlike natural disasters that primarily impact people in one physical location, this virus is taking lives on every corner of the earth. This is a biological tragedy that spares no one. While some are more vulnerable physically, and others are feeling the severe pain of this time financially in exponential ways, ultimately the virus knows no bounds of race, gender, nationality, or social location. A virus that most likely started in a market on the other side of the planet has reminded us that we are all impacted by one another. No one is separate. For better or worse, through sickness and health, richer or poorer, *we are in this together.*

While the stories in this book most often include physical presence, we are learning how to connect without being in proximity to one another. We are finding ways to support our neighbors that involve dropping bags of groceries on porches *after wiping down with Clorox wipes*. We are pushing our political leaders to prioritize those without homes who are crowded into shelters, and to refuse to fall to Darwinian notions of survival of the fittest when we are building public health directives. Parents are slowing down and learning how to support children's schooling from home. Teachers are staying up late, learning new technology, and ensuring that the kids whom they normally care for in the classroom are receiving much needed food and support at home. Faith communities are rallying to learn to conduct Easter services online and to hold Zoom Seder and Iftar meals. As we heed the call to stay home, we are not staying apart. We are finding ways to *connect* in the midst of this time of physical division. As my family stands in the kitchen cooking together, grieving losses one moment, and laughing at a funny movie line, Tiktok, or meme the next, I feel a deep sense of gratitude for the time we would not have otherwise had. There are surely moments when we are finding the *Holy* in the midst of this *chaos.*

Throughout this book, I place this time of ours in context, religiously and politically, and dive deep into the very personal realities and struggles of finding a way forward in multiple contexts with integrity and *love.* I dig into the history of the interactions between religion and politics to help understand from where some of our fears and old patterns come. From the trenches, I share stories of getting it *wrong,* and getting it *right.* As I send this for print, in the midst of coronavirus, I am struggling to see how anything that was relevant before is relevant now. But the truth is, the need to create space for connection crosses time and context. We continue to be impacted by religion and politics and we continue to navigate finding connection in the midst of divisions. In everything I write here, my goal is to spark our imaginations as we move forward together and begin to wonder what might happen if we brought our full loving selves into the difficult, holy, and chaotic political spaces of life.

I realize we are also each in the midst of the chaos of daily life even when there is not a pandemic. Here was the scene when I initially wrote this Prelude: I am currently sitting in a chair, next to my bookshelves, with a big dog half by my side and half on my lap. Three teenagers crisscross through the room, interrupting my clear and (of course!) profound thoughts to complain about a teacher or cry about a friend. My husband stops as he walks through and asks who is picking up kids from school tomorrow and reminds me that our son has a basketball tournament this weekend. We need groceries and toilet paper, and it looks like chocolate milk was spilled on my son's nightstand—at least a week ago. I have twenty baby chicks I am raising in the garage, two jobs I am sure I am neglecting, and a world outside that frequently feels completely overwhelming. I often feel scattered and disoriented as I move from one world to another. This week, as I was about to walk into the State Capitol to testify on a bill to end the death penalty in Colorado, I was informed I was wearing mismatched shoes.

Each day monumental issues with life-and-death consequences progress through the Colorado legislature or pop up on the latest news alert. Each day I wrestle with the realities of white privilege and systemic racism, which I feel in my bones. I am deeply concerned about our society's divisions around critical issues of sexuality, reproductive rights, racism, the environment, immigration, islamophobia and antisemitism, economic inequality, poverty, homelessness, gun violence, mass consumerism, and more. Each and every day I wonder how I can find my place in the daily work to dismantle these toxic realities, and each day I wrestle with how to love my own extended family, particularly those with radically different views.

Life is chaotic.

Life is also holy.

I have come to believe that finding peace in the midst of the chaos is what our lives must be about. Finding connections in the midst of the division. Experiencing healing between the breaths of exhaustion and suffering. Working for ways of loving—personally and systemically—in the midst of the overwhelming fear, anger, and division that swirl around us.

There are no clear maps for this work, but there are practices. There are centuries of people who have come before us whose lives were just as chaotic, overwhelming, and painful, if not more so, and who yet managed to work for survival and thriving in their families and in their communities. They left legacies of resilience, spoke up for what is right, and put their bodies in the places that were needed to move our communities toward justice.

When it comes down to it, I believe we must seek to *love* in challenging spaces. I do not think there are easy answers to this monumental, lifelong task, only a standing invitation to muddle through the holy chaotic task of living together. These words are my way of sharing how I have navigated awkward personal and political spaces, conversations, and work grounded in an inner desire actually to live into the call to *love one another*. The stories I share are my own, and those experiences may differ from the experience of others named in the book. This is long-haul work that is personal and political. It is our job to develop the skills to navigate this chaotic, scary, confusing, and exhilarating territory. It is helpful to know that we are not alone, that we can hold grace with ourselves and others throughout the process. That's what this book is about: the daily work of creating connection in the midst of the real and difficult work that must be done to build the world and the communities for which we yearn.

I hope that these words inspire both reflection and action. Creating connection and boldly entering the worlds of faith and politics takes practice. I have found freedom and creativity through gaining understanding about our historical and current religious and political context. By becoming rooted in our own stories and perspectives on faith and politics, we can explore the fear we have about entering contentious spaces. We can build courage and resilience to step in and show up again and again, even when, inevitably, we mess up from time to time. Through finding joy in one another, we can experience the incredible gift of deep connection, especially across our differences.

Know that you are not alone in this daily work of loving one another. I hope you will come to see the worlds of *faith* and *politics* as less scary and more vital in our commitment to live into the clearest tenets of Christianity—to love God and to love one another—that echo in all major religious traditions. May we develop the skills, habits, practices, and ways of being to find the holy in the midst of the chaos as we enter the most challenging spaces of life together.

* * * *

I begin by laying the groundwork for our shared labor with definitions, as defined by *Merriam-Webster* and me.

holy

- exalted or worthy of complete devotion as one perfect in goodness and righteousness

- having a divine quality, venerated as or as if sacred

- *My definition*: the connection to that which is *beyond*. The sense that something is more significant than a moment; the realization that *"surely, God is in this place."*

chaos

- a state of utter confusion, the unorganized state of primordial matter before the creation of distinct forms

- the inherent unpredictability in the behavior of a complex natural system (such as the atmosphere, boiling water, or the beating heart)

- *My definition*: an anxiety-producing feeling of instability, disorientation. When things are moving so fast, it is challenging to step back, think, breathe, and gain perspective.

faith

- belief and trust (in something sacred, for example, God)

- belief in the traditional doctrines of a religion or a system of religious beliefs

- firm belief in something for which there is no proof

- *My definition:* a deep trust and practice that points us toward God. Faith is concerned with the systems, theories, and rituals that undergird and define a religious belief or practice. Ultimately, for me, faith looks like actions that are grounded in a deeply held belief and commitment to core values or religious teachings. I am less concerned with what your religion *is* and more concerned with what your religion *does*. How do your religious beliefs shape the way you move through the world?

politics

- the art or science of government

- the competition between interest groups or individuals for power and leadership

- the total complex of relations between people living in a society

- *My definition:* the art of navigating life together. This art includes negotiation and decision making to determine the rules and boundaries that support shared experience in personal and public realms.

daily

- occurring, made or acting upon every day

- *My definition:* concerned with the everyday commitment to particular actions. Grounded in resilience and the pragmatic necessity of the long-haul, persistent, recurring needs of living.

love

- strong affection for another arising out of kinship or personal ties

- affection based on admiration, benevolence, or common interests

- warm attachment, enthusiasm, or devotion

- unselfish loyal and benevolent concern for the good of another

- *My definition:* a relationship that is *mutual* and *generative*, and moves toward *justice* in the world. Through nurture, love happens between people; in families and chosen families; with neighbors and communities; between strangers; in cities, states, countries, and political systems.

Peace does not mean

to be free of noise, trouble or hard work,

but to be *in the midst* of those things

and still be calm in your heart.

—*Unknown Author*

1

I *Still* Love You:
Getting to the Heart of the Matter

Standing on the rocky shore overlooking La Jolla Bay, I was observing pupping season in the bay, a time when dozens of seals come to the harbor to have their babies in a place free of predators. The day before, I had literally seen a seal birthing her pup on the beach. I had been watching the mama lying in the sand when suddenly there was a mess at her side including a brand new pup the size of a small dog, and a placenta, which quickly became fodder for the gulls battling overhead.

Today, it was time for swimming lessons. Mama seals and their pups dotted the bay, diving and bobbing. The mamas guided their pups up onto their backs and then let them slide back into the water. They alternately pushed the pups away and pulled them close with their flippers. I watched with delight, laughing aloud and full of awe. Then I noticed that unusually one of the mamas seemed to have two babies with her. Ah, there was another mama close by who must go with the additional pup. Suddenly the two-pup mama noticed the intruder and reared up, snarling and snapping and aggressively pushing herself away from the wandering pup. Startled, the wanderer returned to its own mama where it was quickly reprimanded and then coddled.

For me, it was a startling moment. The placid and loving mama turned so quickly into an angry defender. Of course, most animals do not accept those who are not of their own womb or their own pack. When they do, it makes the news. Remember Koko and her kittens? Taking in young who are not "of our pack" is typically a uniquely human endeavor. Perhaps caring for someone who is "not us" as much as we care for ourselves—with deep, generous care, compassion, and love—is an aspect of our human evolution.

* * * *

The moment with the seals yanked me back to my first moments and days as an adoptive mother. My husband and I had made the decision to adopt out of love. We had experienced the pregnancy and childbirth of "biological children," and we felt we had more to give. We had been in a social justice Bible study group discussing globalization and poverty around the world. We were immersed in books about broken lives and broken systems. We also had long connections to the Philippines, the country where my husband was born at Clark Air Force Base. Lying in bed one night, with three-year-old and one-year-old daughters tucked safely in their respective beds, Kyle and I looked at each other and said nearly simultaneously, "We should adopt." A piece of me knew this would be a more challenging route, but I thought I was up for it.

It was a sunny Monday morning, two years after that bedtime moment, when we got the call. I literally fell to my knees, feeling the gravity of the moment. We had been matched with a healthy little boy who had just turned one year old. He had been brought to a hospital in Bacolod City in the Philippines at about five days old. The hospital staff had searched without success for his birth mother or family. They had spent six months looking for a home for the boy in the Philippines, where one in four people live in desperate poverty, and where there are far more people than available resources. My most sincere prayer was that he had been held and loved through this time, and indeed he had been. At the same time, our broken and imbalanced world left no other options at that moment, and so he was added to the orphanage's list of children looking for homes overseas. We were the lucky family chosen to love and care for him.

We arrived in Bacolod City on August 13, 2007, the morning after a quick flight from Manilla. It was warm and muggy as we drove to the orphanage. The sights and smells were familiar from our travels to other countries where poverty and life intermingle: the crowing of roosters and humming of motorcycle engines, the intermingling acrid and delicious smells of fires and street food, the colorful, clamorous vendors and markets lining the roads.

When we finally pulled up to the "Holy Infant Nursery Foundation," my stomach fluttered with anticipation and nerves. Nursery staff invited us into the large room lined with cribs and cots. I looked into the wooden crib with peeling blue paint and no mattress and saw our baby wearing mint green shorts with a white tank top. He held a small pillow by his side. I knew those little feet from the picture we had been sent. I leaned into the crib and lifted his body to mine and held him for the first time, with tears running down my cheeks.

I held him for the next three hours as we waited for paperwork to be completed, and we dropped off suitcases full of clothes and toys and baby formula sent with us by our loving community back home. When all was complete, we said goodbye to Holy Infant Nursery, climbed in a jeepney, and began the next leg of our journey as a family.

The days and months that followed were filled with wonder, joy, confusion, and exhaustion. Our sweet boy seemed to bond quickly, but my heart was more challenging to crack. I was tired and sick (I had contracted giardia and hepatitis A after our trip), and that added to the challenge of raising three young children. In the months that followed, I learned things about myself I had never known and didn't really want to know. I learned that I become angry and impatient and even have aggressive thoughts. The "self" I had imagined did not show up. Instead, a stranger took my place, a stranger who was depressed, disconnected, and overwhelmed. In that first year, I was forced to face my own demons, to accept that I was not the person or mother I had hoped I would be, and that my expectations were unrealistic and unattainable. These feelings mixed with immense guilt and profound responsibility for the amazing ones in my care. My heart broke.

My heart was broken by the realization of both my own inability to live into my expectations, and the painful realities in the world of poverty, imbalance, injustice, and exploitation, realities that daily affect the lives of individuals, families, and communities.

It took me a good while to come to terms with my broken heart.

Yet it was also during this time of brokenness that I came to live what one of my favorite thinkers, Parker Palmer, speaks about in his theories around the broken heart. Parker Palmer says:

> There are at least two ways to picture a broken heart, using heart in its original meaning not merely as the seat of the emotions but as the core of our sense of self. The conventional image, of course, is that of a heart broken by unbearable tension into a thousand shards—shards that sometimes become shrapnel aimed at the source of our pain. Every day, untold numbers of people try to "pick up the pieces," some of them taking grim satisfaction in the way the heart's explosion has injured their enemies. Here the broken heart is an unresolved wound that we too often inflict on others.

> But there is another way to visualize what a broken heart might mean. Imagine that small, clenched fist of a heart "broken open" into the largeness of life, into a higher capacity to hold one's own and the world's pain and joy. This, too, happens every day. Who among us has not seen evidence, in our own or other people's lives, that compassion and grace can be the fruits of great suffering? Here heartbreak becomes a source of healing, enlarging our empathy and extending our ability to reach out.[1]

When my heart broke open, I became raw, vulnerable, free, and newly able to see the broader brokenness in the world. I asked fresh questions. I sought understanding in books and ideas and stories and in understanding the pain in the world with eyes wide open. During this time, I wound up feeling the call to seminary and to a new vocation—out of deep curiosity about life, meaning, and why the world is the way it is. Ultimately, my broken heart allowed me to see with new eyes and left me with a powerful, persistent longing to be in solidarity with the brokenhearted of the world.

---

[1]Parker Palmer, *The Politics of the Brokenhearted: On Holding the Tensions of Democracy (Essays on Deepening the American Dream)*, (Kalamazoo, Mich.: Fetzer Institute, 2008): 232, available online at https://www.couragerenewal.org/PDFs/Parker-Palmer_politicsbrokenhearted.pdf.

* * * *

Back to the seals teaching the pups to swim in La Jolla Bay. As I watched the mama seal attack the other baby seal, I was both shocked and relieved. Relieved that I was not alone. For loving is hard work. At times we are not our best selves. We hurt and are angry and protective in ways that are not life-supporting. And it is ok. What I felt at that moment with the seals was grace. Loving outside of ourselves goes against thousands of years of training to guard ourselves and others. This loving outside of ourselves is the work of evolving to our deeper humanity. As I experienced through bringing a child into full inclusion and love from outside myself to inside myself, this is difficult and long-haul work. In the process, we learn things about ourselves that we really don't want to know. Our hearts become broken. At our best, in that brokenness we become vulnerable to the pain, life, love, and joy that comes when we open our hearts and eyes to *love beyond.*

* * * *

Ultimately, loving beyond ourselves is the life task to which we are called, isn't it? This is the central teaching in so many of our major religions. The Christian call to love our neighbor as ourselves is similarly stated in each gospel. We can find versions of the great commandment in Matthew 22:35–40, Luke 10:25–28, John 13:31–35 and in Mark 12:28–31. In the Gospel of Mark, Jesus is asked, "Which commandment is the most important of all?" and Jesus answers, "The most important is, 'Hear, O Israel: The Lord our God, the Lord is one. And you shall love the Lord your God with all your heart and with all your soul and with all your mind and with all your strength.' The second is this: 'You shall love your neighbor as yourself.' There is no other commandment greater than these" (Mk. 12:29–31, ESV).

This wasn't something Jesus invented. The commandment quotes from and builds upon the Jewish text, *The Shema*, from Deuteronomy 6:4, the most important Jewish teaching of all. It's so important, one is supposed to recite it in the morning when one wakes and right before closing one's eyes at night. These are the words to be remembered when one passes through a doorway, and each time one prays:

The Lord God is one. Love the Lord with all your heart, all your mind, all your soul.

This is the key to liberation and the key to moving into our shared humanity—to look beyond oneself, to connect to God, and to the liberation of one another.

In a clear parallel, in Surah 4:36 of the Qur'an we find the same simple but profound sentiment: "Serve Allah, and join not any partners with Him; and do good—to parents, kinsfolk, orphans, those in need, neighbors who are near, neighbors who are strangers, the companion by your side, the wayfarer" (Yusuf Ali). The Hadith (or sayings of the Prophet) likewise reminds us, "None of you will have faith until he loves for his brother or his neighbor what he loves for himself" (Sahih Bukhari, Book 2, Hadith 13, https://abuaminaelias.com/dailyhadithonline/2011/03/18/love-brother-neighbor-self/).

In Hinduism, though the word *namaste* has become common and perhaps overused (turned into bumper stickers and t-shirts), it nonetheless speaks the most profound truth: Recognize the divine light in oneself as equal to the divine light in another. The sacred Hindu scriptures, the Upanishads, instructs followers to greet one another upon meeting and parting with the simple and powerful word and motion of *namaste*. This greeting is a visceral reminder that we are connected. Saying the word *namaste* recognizes that the life force, the divinity, the Self, or the God in me is the same in *all*. In acknowledging this oneness and equality by putting our palms together in greeting, we honor God in the person we meet.

Similarly, the African traditional spiritual teaching of *ubuntu* reminds us that "I am because we are," expressing the most profound truth toward others and the belief in a universal bond of sharing that connects all humanity. The teaching of *ubuntu* states that to be human is to affirm one's humanity by recognizing the humanity of others and, on that basis, to establish respectful human relations with them. A person is a person only through other people. We create each other and need each other. In belonging to each other, we participate in our mutual creation: we are because you are, and since you are, I am. Across traditions, across time, we are called to love...beyond.

* * * *

We know this, the call to love our neighbor as ourselves. We have heard it many times. But do we *live it?* Do we live it in our personal lives with those with whom we walk through life? Do we live it in our communities and our cities? Do we live this call to love in our political lives?

I believe that this central idea of loving our neighbor as ourselves is a core teaching in most of our religious traditions precisely because loving one another—genuinely loving one another across all of our differences in our daily lives—is so incredibly hard. We need to hear it again and again in different languages, through various traditions, and different teachers: Love God, and love one another as ourselves.

Throughout time, we humans have tackled and found ways forward through some of the most intractable dilemmas that have confronted us. We discovered that wheels not only helped speed the production of pottery, but could facilitate the transport of both objects and people. We found that penicillin could stop infections and prevent people from dying from toothaches and minor cuts as well as more serious ailments. We created calendars and mechanical clocks to track time and organize ourselves across multiple locations. We mastered flight to take us from one end of the world to the other in a matter of hours. We discovered that we could harness electricity to provide light in the night, to sustain energy, to wire our homes, and ultimately to shape life as we know it.

And yet, we still can't figure out how to solve one of the most entrenched and basic obstacles in all of human history: how to help people love one another. How can we build genuine care about the survival, well-being, and thriving of those who are "not us"? How do we cultivate responsibility for their daily lives and opportunities, and grow this care regardless of circumstances—meaning regardless of what they think and how they see the world, regardless of the choices they have made in the past or are making now. How do we care about their well-being as much as we care about our own—no matter where they were born or whom they love? How do we work both to "see" them and to treat them with dignity in our personal interactions and systemically by assuring that our laws, policies, and cultural norms also support their survival, well-being, and thriving? This requires seeing, hearing, listening, imagining, letting go, and wondering.

How we convince people genuinely to care about one another—really love and care about one another as much as we love and care about ourselves and our families—is an intractable problem we have not yet figured out. We have done it neither in our daily interactions and life together nor in our political systems.

* * * *

When I use the words *love* and *politics* in the same sentence, most of us have a guttural reaction of discomfort. Add *religion* to the mix, and we have some real trouble! Yet given that the central tenet in Christianity and in each of our great religious traditions is to love, shouldn't this shape the way we live together personally and politically? Love is *not* lawlessness or anarchy. Love does not make us a softy pushover. Love is a posture, a way of being in the world that honors the deepest humanity of the other. Love is a commitment to seeking the well-being and thriving for the other as much as we seek that for ourselves.

Loving beyond ourselves is the lifelong, revolutionary journey of work to which we are called. That journey starts with us. In the process of trying to love "the other," we learn things about ourselves that we really didn't want to know—much as I learned uncomfortable things about myself when we adopted our son. Yet step into uncomfortable places we must. And because of that, our hearts will be broken, our egos will be humbled, and our resilience will be tested.

In my first year as an adoptive mother, I realized that such loving is so much harder than I thought it was going to be, and that *I was the only obstacle*. For me, realizing my deep desire and commitment to care for these children I loved and acknowledging my own shortcomings prompted me to get my act together. I embarked on a journey to do my personal spiritual and reflective work so that I could care for our three beautiful children. Through these experiences, my eyes were opened to how this learning to love beyond would shape the ways I build relationships with people from multiple religious, racial, cultural, and political backgrounds, and would develop my ways of working for political and systemic transformation.

* * * *

Five years ago, I found myself working in a place I hadn't fully expected to be in—at the intersection of faith and politics in one of the more divisive times in recent American history. When I began working with the Interfaith Alliance of Colorado, I had no idea of the incredible opportunities for learning and growth I would find. Yes, we are in a time when our differences are being exploited, and often we are pitted or pit ourselves against the other. There's nothing new about this. Our country was built on dehumanizing and exploiting people based on differences in skin color, language, and culture. Tribalism and us-and-them thinking are deeply embedded in our American psyche.

This truth had been relatively easy for me to avoid, as an able-bodied, straight, white, Christian woman—that is until I started to enter spaces where the pain of our history and our time were unavoidable, and where my call as a Christian to work for mutual liberation was too insistent. In the past five years, the seed that was planted through my experience of adopting a child and learning to love beyond has taken root in the daily work of building relationships across radical difference, and through a commitment to the long-haul work of living into the hopes we share for personal and systemic transformation and liberation.

As I walk through the halls of power and sit in hearings listening to the sausage-making of democracy in the form of people's stories of hope, pain, and desire for systems that will support our connected lives, I am humbled by both our collective human pain and hope. It certainly seems at times that we are living in entirely different worlds from the worlds of those with whom we disagree on critical issues. However, we can find small points of our more profound humanity in a moment of eye contact, or a laugh about our little mistakes, or a need to stop to share a sandwich amid a long, contentious meeting. In working with people and organizations who come with varying interests and radically different life experiences, I have learned that when it comes down to it, we are each trying to survive the days. We are seeking love in our personal lives and seeking friends who "get" us. We are worried about our children. We are frustrated when we get stuck in traffic or can't seem to arrive at the next place on time.

But some of us have very different obstacles. Some people are prevented from thriving by systemic realities that keep them from getting loans or education or healthcare, or from being able to afford the ridiculous rent for a one-bedroom apartment. Some hold the scars of abuse or carry the burden of generational trauma and suffering. Others have grown accustomed to being able to get what they want when they want it and have lost sight of those who are harmed by their desires. These are realities that must be seen, understood, and addressed. I now recognize that the only way we will find true healing and mutual liberation is by caring for one another, by observing the full humanity of those with whom we are working—and even those against whom we are working.

* * * *

One evening, when my son was about five years old, I tucked the bedcovers up over his little chest and under his chin. It had been a rough day. I am sure he had had a tantrum about something or other, and I am sure I had had a tantrum as well. I don't recall what had led to the blow-up, but I do remember the exhaustion and exasperation. I leaned down to kiss his forehead, and he looked me in the eyes and said: "Mom, I *still* love you." A wave of breath moved through my body. I call it grace. I paused and said, "I *still* love you too, buddy." Never in all my life had I felt such love and acceptance in the midst of the messiness and pain. I have come to see that *this* is the heart of the matter. As we enter the painful realities of living together, we are called to wade through and love each other *still*. We are called to keep working for what's right. To keep speaking up, to keep reaching out. To listen, reflect, learn, think. To mess up, to win, to lose. And in the midst of it all, the first step in building relationships across our differences is to remember this central call: *to love each other, still.*

Love is like a lawsuit

I am amazed at the seeker of purity

who when it's time to be polished

complains of rough handling.

Love is like a lawsuit:

to suffer harsh treatment is the evidence;

when you have no evidence, the lawsuit is lost.

Don't grieve when the Judge demands your evidence;

kiss the snake so that you may gain the treasure.

That harshness isn't toward you,

but toward the harmful qualities within you.

When someone beats a rug,

the blows are not against the rug,

but against the dust in it.

—Rumi

Questions for Reflection

1. What were you taught about love?

2. What did your religious upbringing teach you about loving your neighbors? Your enemies? How does this relate to political life?

3. What feelings arise in your body when you hear the words *religion* and *politics*?

4. When have you struggled to "love beyond yourself?"

5. How are you experiencing the current political climate in your family? Community?

6. What do you need to navigate religious and political conversations better?

2

First Things First: Seeking to Understand

I stepped onto the airplane with my neck pillow and blanket in hand, preparing myself for the long flight ahead. I was heading to Tel Aviv for a two-week trip through Israel and Palestine to learn about the conflict in the Middle East and efforts to work for peace. Just as we were getting ready to take off, I noticed a row of men standing in the back of the plane refusing the flight attendant's requests to find their seats. They were wearing what I learned are *tallit* (a Jewish prayer shawl) and *tefillin* (leather straps and a box containing scrolls with scripture), their *payot* (side hair in curls) dangling down the sides of their faces from beneath their black hats. I was taken aback by the bold way in which the men (only men) refused to sit in their airline seats and insisted they had to perform their evening prayers. I watched the flight attendants make trips back and forth between the pilots in the front and the men praying in the back—until the flight crew finally gave up and delayed the flight. We all waited on the tarmac until they were done. The men were on their way home to Israel, the land they consider to be the God-ordained Jewish state. For these Orthodox Jews, the state and religion were one; religious law should override any civil law—apparently even the laws of the U.S. Federal Aviation Administration. What I witnessed that day on the plane to Israel was an expression of Judaism that was very different from that of the Jewish friends I had come to know at that point. I was struck by their deep commitment and by the way this commitment bumped up against the hopes of the rest of us to get the long flight underway.

Through this experience, I came to see that there are many ways to navigate religion and the laws of the land. I also understood the truth of the statement, "If you meet *one* Jewish person, you have met *one* Jewish person." Likewise, if you meet *one* Muslim or *one* Christian, then you have met *one* Muslim or *one* Christian. Within each religion are diverse teachings and practices, and diverse teachings about how to engage with "the world" through politics. There is as much diversity of thought and action within each tradition as there is between traditions. Within and between each of our religions are multiple ways of engaging political life.

This was a big learning curve for me. Growing up, I assumed everyone was Christian like me. I knew nothing else. I went to high school in north Colorado Springs, home of the conservative Christian media organization Focus on the Family. I thought *all* Christians were conservative and Republican, stood against abortion and gay rights, and drove minivans with fish symbols proudly displayed above the bumper. I skipped the Fellowship of Christian Athletes gatherings before school and politely declined to attend youth group at my friends' churches. Although my family was certainly culturally Christian, my parents rejected the dogma of the institutional church. Much of it just didn't seem right to me, but I didn't have the words to explain why.

I did not actually meet anyone who shared that they were not Christian until after college when I moved to Cleveland to do an internship at the Cleveland Clinic to become a Registered Dietitian. I am sure I had met people before this who were not Christian, but it had never been a point of conversation. My first night in Cleveland, I gathered with the other interns, who had come from across the country for the same internship. Together we ventured into town to go to the Slavic Festival. I am reasonably sure I had never heard the word *Slavic* before. I shocked my new friends when I shared that this was my first taste of pierogi, the delicious doughy potato-and-cheese-filled Polish staple. I moved through the rows of vendors with excitement and awe, experiencing Eastern European culture, food, religion, art, and music for the first time.

The next evening I had everyone over to my apartment to continue getting to know one another. As my new friends scoped out my apartment and browsed the books on my shelves (the best way to get to know a person!), someone noted that I must *really* like the Bible. I wasn't sure what they were talking about. They noted that I had *six* Bibles on my shelf, something I hadn't thought twice about. They made a couple of jokes about how religious I was, even though I wasn't at the time, and then everyone opened up about their religious backgrounds. A few people didn't grow up religious, one person was Lutheran, another was Catholic, and one said he was Jewish. My ears perked up, and I riddled him with questions. This was the first time I had met someone who was Jewish (or at least who had shared that they were Jewish). I was fascinated and grateful for the new relationships that were opening my eyes to different ways of believing and moving through the world. This experience sparked my desire to keep learning. Over time and with years of experiences and new relationships, I became aware of the enormous diversity of religions present in the U.S. today.

In addition to meeting people who identified as Jewish, Muslim, Buddhist, Hindu, and so forth, I learned—perhaps most surprisingly to me—that there are liberal Christians. I learned that these liberal Christians are also *real* Christians who have roots both in Christianity in America and in Christianity across the globe since the beginning of the life and teachings of Christ. At the time this rocked my world. Quite often I see this same sense of confusion on people's faces when I speak and act out of the Christianity I follow as a woman who often wears a clergy collar and who has more progressive political views.

As an American society, we have minimal experience of or historical perspective on the vast diversity of religious beliefs, practices, histories, and cultures present in the United States. We have very little understanding of the ways this diversity and history shape our daily lives and political realities. Gaining insight and perspective into the history of religion and politics in the U.S. and beyond has given me a sense of freedom to bring my full self into these vital spaces. Learning about the history and diversity of religion and politics is not simply an academic exercise; for me it has become an avenue through which to explore the questions that can guide us as I move in divisive religious and political worlds today.

Religion and Politics

Indeed, it seems we humans are living in different, separate worlds. At the root of these differences are divergent worldviews and different understandings of history, truth, and religion. We debate the core values of our country and our communities, with each "side" believing their way reflects the "original intent" of the founders of our country—and is therefore inherently superior. Debates play out in school curricula and on TV news shows alike. How we understand the past shapes how we live into the future. If we believe that the U.S. was formed as a "Christian nation" prioritizing "Christian" norms, this shapes how we believe our laws and policies should play out. If we believe that the separation of church and state, and the ideal of pluralism and diversity of thought and belief are woven into our Constitution, we approach the changing demographics of our country and shifting laws in particular ways. When we step into the contentious spaces of religion and politics, it is helpful to understand the context of the two in our shared American history.

I have come to understand that religion has always been political, and that politics has always been religious. How the two have related to each other has varied widely. While the goal of politics has primarily been to form our shared life using power, resources, and laws, there have always been intertwined relationships between politics and religion(s) of "the people." Religion can be defined as the set of beliefs and practices that a person or group of people follow.[1] This inherently affects shared political life. Historically, and in some places currently, people use religion even more than national and country boundaries to define land and territories. Sometimes the dominant religion is tied to the political structures, and at other times religions are at odds with or oppressed by political power holders. Usually, it's somewhere in the middle of these two extremes.

From the earliest Mesopotamian civilizations that regarded religion, politics, and the natural world as intimately connected and determining daily survival to texts of the Hebrew Bible that describe kings chosen by God to rule the people, we see a dynamic relationship between religious beliefs and political practices. From

---

[1]The definition of religion itself is certainly contested. Religion as a term was not understood in the ways we use it today until after the Enlightenment. The term *religion* has been shaped by political and social forces.

the prophets who spoke the truth in the face of power against the corruption of kings and rulers to the threat Jesus was to the political forces that ruled Rome, religious powers variously supported and challenged political rule.

Some religions, or branches within religions, teach followers to stay out of our shared political life. There are strains within Christianity, Judaism, Islam, Taoism, Hinduism, and Buddhism that reject politics for several reasons, including the view that politics is divisive, concerned with the artificial, and prone to corruption. Some people within the Chinese philosophy of Taoism have rejected political involvement out of a belief that a life of contemplation in nature is preferable. Some Christian traditions, such as Jehovah's Witnesses, the Amish, and the Exclusive Brethren, admonish followers to avoid politics altogether; they believe that Christ's statements about the differences between the kingdom of God and the kingdom of the world cannot be reconciled. Some religious sects, such as the Nation of Islam, have often rejected American politics out of a belief that the entire system is corrupt and irredeemable.

In contrast, some religions, or traditions within religions, specifically instruct followers to participate actively in the shared political life. As I learned from my friend Dilpreet, who is himself engaged in local school board and city leadership and who has raised his daughters to be vocal and active leaders in the community, one of the core tenets of Sikhism is a specific instruction to participate in civic life. The first Sikh people came from India to the U.S. in the late nineteenth century. In 1957, Dalip Singh Saund became the first Sikh person elected to political office, serving the District of Columbia. Today, Sikh people serve in positions of public leadership and are active in shared civic life all across the U.S.

If we take a look at local leadership at every level in communities and nationally, we will see people who are Jewish and who lead out of the long tradition of community leadership. My friend Jill speaks of the teaching of *tikkun olam* as her interior inspiration to work for healing and justice in Colorado. Tikkun olam is a cosmological myth created in the sixteenth century by the great Jewish mystic, Rabbi Isaac Luria of Safed, which says that at the beginning of the world a vessel of light was shattered into countless pieces. The call of humanity is to gather these pieces from the four corners of the earth to repair the world.

Tikkun olam is the idea that Jews are responsible not only for their own moral, spiritual, and material well-being but also for the welfare of society at large. For many in the Jewish community, this means participating in political efforts for social justice or even serving in public office. Beyond the more recent reclaiming of the teaching of tikkun olam, Jewish people have participated in political life for centuries and in American political experience since the nation's founding. The first Jewish member of a colonial legislature was Francis Salvador in 1775, and the first Jewish governor was David Emanuel in 1801.

Among Christians, some people are motivated by Christian teachings to be the "hands of Christ" in the world, with varying interpretations of what exactly that means. There are Christian people who participate in every level of public life and from different ends of the political spectrum. Growing up, I thought Christian participation in political life simply meant being a Republican. As I became older, I met people who were rooted in the social justice tradition of Christianity. I participated in a Catholic social justice Bible study series called "Just Faith" and learned that there is a long history of Christian leaders engaging in direct work to improve their communities, stand with those experiencing marginalization, and work for systemic change. Reading the works of Dorothy Day and Martin Luther King, Jr., in addition to poets and authors such as Annie Dillard and Parker Palmer, helped me see that for me and many others, being engaged in public life and courageously being involved in political issues is a central call of Christian practice.

The Story of Tikkun Olam[2]

At the beginning of time, God's presence filled the universe. When God decided to bring this world into being, to make room for creation, He first drew in His breath, contracting Himself. From that contraction, darkness was created. And when God said, "Let there be light" (Gen. 1:3), the light that came into being filled the darkness, and ten holy vessels came forth, each filled with primordial light.

---

[2]Howard Schwartz, "How the Ari Created a Myth and Transformed Judaism," *Tikkun* (March 28, 2011), available at https://www.tikkun.org/how-the-ari-created-a-myth-and-transformed-judaism.

In this way God sent forth those ten vessels, like a fleet of ships, each carrying its cargo of light. Had they all arrived intact, the world would have been perfect. But the vessels were too fragile to contain such a powerful, divine light. They broke open, split asunder, and all the holy sparks were scattered like sand, like seeds, like stars. Those sparks fell everywhere, but more fell on the Holy Land than anywhere else.

That is why we were created—to gather the sparks, no matter where they are hidden. God created the world so that the descendants of Jacob could raise up the holy sparks. That is why there have been so many exiles—to release the holy sparks from the servitude of captivity. In this way, the Jewish people will sift all the holy sparks from the four corners of the earth.

And when enough holy sparks have been gathered, the broken vessels will be restored, and tikkun olam, the repair of the world, awaited so long, will finally be complete. Therefore it should be the aim of everyone to raise these sparks from wherever they are imprisoned and to elevate them to holiness by the power of their soul.

Politics and Religion

After September 11, 2001, fear and misinformation spread false claims that Muslim people would follow the mysterious Sharia law above the U.S. Constitution. Since that time, seven states in the United States have officially banned Sharia law. This fear shows ignorance about Sharia law, which provides a foundation to guide Muslims in living their lives, much as the Jewish law or the teachings of Christianity guide Jews and Christians, and it portrays an ignorance of the U.S. Constitution and the relationship between religion and government. I have heard my friend Iman (which means "faith" in Arabic) respond to questions about Sharia law countless times in her Islam 101 trainings around our community. According to Muslim law, and similar to the Judaic and Christian commandments, followers of Islam are instructed to follow the law of the land in which they live. Some things which are *haram,* or forbidden, in Islam are legal according to U.S. law, such as drinking alcohol or eating pork, but a Muslim person would never expect a non-Muslim person to follow Islamic law. Democratic laws have been built on ethical and moral principles that have their foundation in many of our religious traditions, but which have all been agreed upon and deemed to be shared laws by a secular state, laws such as "Do not murder."

* * * *

Four primary relationships between religion and politics can be seen historically and to this day: (1) theocracy, (2) state religion, (3) the secular state (separation of church and state), and (4) state hostility toward religious institutions. The most common form of government tied to religion in early civilizations were theocracies. In a theocracy, a religious institution is the source of all authority in the government, and a religious ruler rules in the name of a god. Most countries in the West ended theocratic rule after the Enlightenment. Today, theocratic governments remain in places such as Saudi Arabia, Afghanistan, Iran, and Vatican City. A theocratic rule can be tempting because it is efficient, as it has little tolerance for diversity or debate. A theocratic government can also be oppressive, likewise, because there is little tolerance for diversity or debate.

State religions are government-sanctioned establishments of a religion, but the state does not need to be under the control of the religion (as in a theocracy), nor is the state-sanctioned religion necessarily under the power of the state. The state religion is a religion officially endorsed by the state, and it can take multiple forms. Most monarchies have some level of state religion. State religions can simply be an endorsement of a particular religion with no doctrinal or financial exchange, or they can involve financial support, including state funding of religious houses of worship or salaries for clergy people paid by tax dollars. Germany, for example, to this day collects taxes directly from people who identify as Lutheran and pays the salaries of Lutheran pastors out of these taxes.

Some countries with state-sanctioned religions allow other faiths to practice, and support religious diversity within the country, such as modern England, Germany, Malaysia, and Morocco. There are Jewish states, such as Israel, and Islamic states, such as Egypt, Bahrain, and Jordan, that have a state designated religion, but allow the practice of other religions. According to Pew Research Center, more than four in ten countries around the world endorse or favor a specific religion. Islam is endorsed by twenty-seven countries, and thirteen endorse Christianity. Forty countries favor a particular religion, mostly Christianity. Favoring a religion, means there is not a legal endorsement, but there are legal and cultural assumptions that favor one particular religion. In contrast, some countries are hostile to non-state religions and religious freedom—such as North Korea, Somalia, and Syria—and they prohibit the practice of any competing religion and/or actively persecute followers of other sects.

Secular states are, in theory, countries that have not claimed an official state religion or favored religion. Most secular states allow freedom of religious practice, and most work to prevent state entanglement with one religion over another. The U.S. is a secular state with freedom of religion, though in reality this is clearly in constant negotiation. Compared to formal relationships between political and religious institutions, the facts on the ground may be very different from the ideals in each of the various relational agreements. For example, although the U.S. was founded on an idea of religious pluralism and diversity, some people argue that the U.S. is a Christian nation, and there are people who believe that the culture should be defined religiously even if it is not named as such constitutionally. Of course, this raises questions as to which version of Christianity that state would follow. All of this is important information: It is helpful to know where we came from, who we want to be, and who we *don't* want to be.

Religion and Politics in the United States

In my first months working with the Interfaith Alliance of Colorado, I learned that a gay couple, Charlie and Dave, had been refused service by a baker at Masterpiece Cake Shop when they went to the store in search of a wedding cake. A Supreme Court ruling had recently deemed gay marriage to be legal, establishing a new battleground. The baker, Jack Phelps, claimed that his religious freedom was being infringed upon as he did not want to participate (by making a cake) in a marriage that contravened his religious beliefs. Charlie's and Dave's rights were also being infringed upon, as the state of Colorado protects LGBTQ people from being discriminated against in a public business. Over the years, I have spoken on stage with Charlie and Dave, sat with them in legislative hearings, and shared tears and life stories. I have seen the pain it has caused them to be judged and turned away for who they are. Dave speaks of the humiliation of standing with his mom at the bakery counter, excited and overwhelmed as they worked through the details of their wedding, only to be rejected for who he was.

I have also heard Jack Phelps speak about the business he lost for holding on to his deepest convictions. I disagree with the idea that refusing to serve anyone is a Christian belief or ideal, but I do see the underlying conflict that ensues when our core values are put on the line. To understand fully the conflicts that happen when one person's freedom goes head-to-head with another person's freedom, I offer a brief review of how we got here.

When we think back to the earliest religious makeup of the land that would become the United States, many of us conjure up images of Pilgrims and Puritans in black dresses, white aprons, and funny hats fleeing religious persecution in Europe. However, the actual history is far more convoluted. From the start, the religious makeup of people who came together on the land that would become the United States was enormously diverse. First, of course, there were already people living on the land when the first European ships arrived, people who had lived there for millennia, and these Native peoples had deeply held religious beliefs and practices of their own. Next, among those who came to the "New World," there were multiple sects of Christians—yes, including those Pilgrims and Puritans who were fleeing the state religion of the Church of England, and also those who were loyal to the King and Church of England. There were multiple sects of Protestant movements, Roman Catholics who were loyal to the pope, as well as people who were Jewish or who practiced one of many other religions.

In addition, those who were brought to the country as enslaved Africans had their own beliefs and practices. As many as 30 percent of the people who were enslaved are thought to have been practicing Muslims; many others were adherents of traditional African religions, and many of these sought to maintain their religious practice amid oppressive circumstances.

The dominant story of colonial America was of how settlers forming new communities quickly began to replicate theocratic relationships between their preferred religion and civic life. Different Christian sects immediately clashed with one another. Catholic, Jewish, atheist, and Muslim people were subjected to religious intolerance and bigotry. Over time, adherents of new religions likewise became targets of religious persecution. Most significantly, Native people were persecuted, kidnapped, murdered, or violently converted to Christianity and Western culture. The Doctrine of Discovery (a fifteenth-century Papal Bull) and ideas of Manifest Destiny deemed legal and even moral the theft of land and the enslavement and murder of people who were seen as not fully human because they were not "civilized Christians."

By the time of the American Revolution, overlaying the colonies was an intricate quilt of state laws regarding religion.[3] In Massachusetts, only Christians were allowed to hold public office, and Catholics were allowed to do so only after renouncing papal authority. In 1777, New York State's constitution banned Catholics from public office (and would do so until 1806). In Maryland, which was initially founded as a haven for Catholics, Catholics had full civil rights but Jews did not. Public officials in Delaware were required to take an oath affirming belief in the Trinity. In the middle colonies lived people who adhered to a variety of religions, including Quakers (who founded Pennsylvania), Catholics, Lutherans, a few Jews, and others. The southern colonists likewise represented a variety of denominations, including Baptists and Anglicans. The Carolinas and Virginia legally recognized the Church of England as the state church, and a portion of tax revenues went to support its parish and priests. Virginia imposed laws obliging all to attend Anglican public worship.

All of this matters because it was within this context, while faced with options to declare a particular state religion, that the authors of the Constitution and the Bill of Rights wrote what would become a guiding principle in the very first amendment to the Constitution: "Congress shall make no law respecting an establishment of religion, or prohibiting the free exercise thereof; or abridging the freedom of speech, or of the press; or the right of

---

[3]Tisa Joy Wenger. *Religious Freedom: The Contested History of an American Ideal* (Chapel Hill: University of North Carolina Press, 2017).

the people peaceably to assemble, and to petition the Government for a redress of grievances."

Authors of the Bill of Rights were undoubtedly affected by the different expressions of Christianity of their time and by theocratic rule that many had experienced in Europe. They wrote in the context of the First Great Awakening that had instilled an emotional and enthusiastic Christian following in the colonies and was shaped by the Deist and humanist philosophies. At the same time they were seeped in Enlightenment philosophy grounded in reason and a priority of individual freedom and rights. Over the course of time, the country's leaders came to a clear decision that the new country would not be a theocracy, that there would be no favored religion, and that the country would countenance hostility toward no religion but rather would tolerate and support diverse religious beliefs and practices. George Washington, in a letter to a Jewish community navigating life as religious minorities in Rhode Island, said the federal government gave, "to bigotry no sanction, to persecution no assistance."[4]

We continue to muddle through like this today. Freedom of religion was meant to shield people from bigotry, not to harm them. Of course, these high ideals were written in a context that still sanctioned slavery, ignored women, and slaughtered Native peoples. Whenever we are in contentious religious and political spaces, it is helpful to remember that diversity of thought and practice were built into our imperfect democratic system.

That Old-Time Religion

Today when most people think of religion in America, what comes to mind is the form of Christianity that has taken shape since the end of the Second World War, after which there was a steep increase in church attendance and in the building of the institutions of religious denominations. The Christianity that took shape after 1945 had two main streams and built on two

---

[4]George Washington, letter to the Hebrew congregation in Newport, Rhode Island on Wednesday, August 18, 1790, available on the Mount Vernon website at https://www.mountvernon.org/library/digitalhistory/quotes/article/for-happily-the-government-of-the-united-states-which-gives-to-bigotry-no-sanction-to-persecution-no-assistance-requires-only-that-they-who-live-under-its-protection-should-demean-themselves-as-good-citizens-in-giving-it-on-all-occasions-their-effectual-s/ .

divergent impulses from the second Great Awakening of the early nineteenth century. One path was rooted in more liberal views of scripture and culture, the other took a fundamentalist or literal view of scripture and piety and of resistance to cultural change. Amid the shifting culture of the 1960s, including the rise of women's rights, the sexual revolution, and the civil rights movement, a counter-movement formed within the fundamentalist stream of Christianity that married political and religious forces with a call to "return to traditional values" of "God and country" that had been instilled in the early twentieth century. Although this was a *new* movement in Christianity, many people today think this is the one true Christianity and that it is closely aligned with the earliest Christian communities, an idea that is highly debatable.

The 1970s saw the rise of a political and religious movement known as the Religious Right. The Religious Right, led by Evangelical pastors, institutions such as the Moral Majority, the Family Research Council, and my hometown organization Focus on the Family, used media, politics, and churches to promote a version of Christianity that emphasized what they considered to be the "fundamentals" of Christianity. The new movement insisted on the inerrancy of scripture, emphasized so-called "traditional gender roles," countered the newly legal abortion law of Roe vs. Wade, and rejected the movements for LGBTQ equality. This is the Christianity I grew up hearing about from my grandparents in a little Baptist church, surrounded by people whom I regarded as loving. This was the only Christianity I knew until I was in my mid-twenties.

For nearly fifty years, the culture wars of conservative religion vs. secular culture in the U.S. have held power in the media and in our public dialogue and have shaped politics from presidential elections to local school boards and city councils. Hotly debated issues about prayer in school, the placement of the ten commandments in courthouses, the teaching of evolution in our public school curriculums, abortion rights, women's equality, racial equality, and LGBTQ rights have dominated the religious-political landscape. Two generations of Americans have grown up regarding this evangelicalism as the only expression of Christianity, and for many, as the only "true" religion. However, these fights certainly do not tell the whole story of religion in the U.S. today.

Religious diversity in the United States began to increase after the 1965 Immigration and Nationality Act. The influx of people from different countries who brought their religion and culture with them had a direct impact on religious diversity and pluralism in America. According to the Pew Research Center, Christians still make up 70 percent of the population in the U.S. However, the percentage of "Nones" (those who name no religious affiliation) increases with each survey. The percentage of Muslim people in the U.S. increases each year, and according to Pew, the number of births to Muslim parents are expected to overtake the number of births to Christian parents by 2035. More people from non-Christian religious backgrounds are serving in public office across the country than ever before. Christianity itself is wildly diverse: It includes people who are Catholic, Methodist, Evangelical, Pentecostal, Lutheran, Adventist, African Methodist Episcopal, Baptist, Presbyterian—the list of different sects and denominations could fill hundreds of pages. Christian people can be found with different views on every major issue, political or otherwise.

While Christians continue to enjoy disproportionate prominence in public leadership compared to national demographics, as I write in 2020 the U.S. Congress includes people who are Muslim, Jewish, Hindu, Buddhist, Sikh, Unitarian, Orthodox, and who claim no religion. As the assumption of Protestant Christian dominance has decreased, it has left more space for people from multiple religious backgrounds or none at all to enter the public sphere and to influence culture. Whether the religious diversity we experience today is what the founders of the Constitution and the Bill of Rights expected when they penned the words is debatable. However, the idea of a country tied together by a shared commitment to something beyond one particular religion allowed space for the free exercise of religion and planted the seeds of the religious diversity and inclusion we see and hope for today.

At its best, freedom of religion leads to religious pluralism. Religious pluralism is the idea that supports the presence of multiple religious views and practices within society. Pluralism is *not* relativism. No, all religions are *not* the same. Stephen Prothero clarifies in his book *God Is Not One* that saying "We are all the same" perpetuates abusive power structures.[5]

---

[5]Stephen Prothero, *God Is Not One: The Eight Rival Religions That Run the World—and Why Their Differences Matter* (New York: HarperOne, 2010).

When I say "You are just like me," I am actually refusing to *see you* and am instead silencing your voice and experience. So, too, for religion. Pluralism at its deepest level honors and appreciates the full depth of belief, practice, and identity of people who may hold radically different views and ways of living, and it creates space for shared laws and agreements beyond the particulars of our religious commitments. This requires a constant process of navigation.

As we try to live together across religious differences, three questions root the work of navigating church and state relationships:

1. Where does loyalty lie?

   Is our first priority the teachings of our faith or a commitment to the law of the land? Will Catholics follow the Pope or the Constitution? Will Muslims follow Sharia law or local laws? Will the new Americans be loyal to the King of England or to the forming colonies? How can Native Americans reconcile the commanded to assimilate to the cause and culture of their invaders with the centuries of tradition and commitment to their land? Will religious followers fight for the state or refuse to, based on their religion? Will they rebel against the state when they are unhappy?

   This question of where our loyalty lies is at the heart of religious freedom and pluralism in the age of the nation-state. As we embark on connecting across our differences in the realms of faith and politics, we are faced with questions of to whom and to what we are most loyal. Are we loyal to a political party or to values and principles? Are we loyal to the teachings of our faith or to the norms of our society? Are we loyal to a religious sect or denomination or to a commitment to our common humanity? What do we do when the tenets of our faith conflict with the laws of the land?

2. Does the religion support the interests of the state or burden the interests of the state?

   The underlying assumption of this question is that the state is the collective body of people who form the political state. States have many interests, predominantly safety, economic security, cultural unity (not uniformity), and (we hope) the well-being of their citizens. Religious people and organizations do incredible work to support the common good. Religious groups run hospitals, care for those most vulnerable, host food pantries, and serve meals to those who are hungry. Religious institutions found and run universities and schools and provide career training and support. In the U.S., decisions have been made to give state contracts to religiously-based service providers who offer health care, foster homes, or hunger relief services. Each of these actions supports the interests of the state if the state is interested in the welfare of its people. By contrast, religions burden the interests of the state if people or groups refuse to participate in shared laws or agreements. For example, if a Quaker person refuses to participate in war or a Baptist person refuses to pay taxes, this burdens the interests of the state in ensuring that it can defend itself in times of war and achieve economic solvency through taxes.

An argument of burden was used in the aforementioned Masterpiece Cake Supreme Court ruling. The interest of the state is to assure that people can receive goods and services free of discrimination, according to state non-discrimination laws. The baker claimed that his religious freedom is violated by being coerced to bake a wedding cake for a wedding with which he disagrees, in line with his religious beliefs. The legal question underlying the case is: Who is more burdened? Is it the state, which is burdened by not being able to protect citizens from discrimination? Or is it the religious baker, who is burdened by violating his religion by baking a cake?

3. Does religion provide more stability for the state, or does religion disrupt stability?

    Like us, states long for the elusive feeling of stability. Change can feel destabilizing and disorienting, making us feel less safe. Religions can bring stability to people's lives and political systems, or they can be disruptive and destabilizing. Religions often help people live moral, ethical lives; they provide community, support during times of crisis, and rituals that bring meaning and fulfillment. These things create stability for individuals and families, and hence a more stable and peaceful state. However, religions can also inspire people to uproot their lives, give all of their possessions to the poor, remove themselves from economic systems, or point out systemic injustice and chain themselves to an immigration detention facility to protest the immoral actions of a state. These actions can be seen to cause instability in the status quo of a state. Underlying this is the question: stability for whom? Most often, concerns of stability are focused on those who already hold power and already benefit from the status quo.

Arguments were made in the early days of the movement for rights and equality for LGBTQ people that allowing marriage equality would disrupt the stability of the "traditional family." Politicians and political leaders initially bought into these arguments and were slow to change laws or to support rights and equality. This was not only for religious reasons. Some see the traditional family as the building block of social stability. Some people thought that disrupting or diminishing "the family" would destabilize "the state." This might be a valid point if stability were concerned only with those who experience stability in traditional families. A young person who is being treated as less than human, or who is contemplating suicide after being shunned by their family, or who feels the pain of rejection is not stable in a status quo that refuses their right to exist. In working at the intersection of religion and politics, it is helpful to be aware of who is experiencing stability through our beliefs and actions, and who is not.

Politics, Religion, and Me

Religion and politics evoke difficult conversations about what we believe and how we want to live our lives. Most often, these questions involve messy and convoluted realities. Perhaps this is why we are taught from a young age that because conflicts inevitably ensue, religion and politics are two topics to avoid at all costs. The questions require thought and reflection as we confront our own assumptions. Rather than engage in the challenging work of thoughtfully entering the worlds of religion and politics, many of us pretend that these two worlds don't affect our daily lives. But in doing so, we hand over our power to those who are quite happy to enter both arenas, and we accept the status quo— or worse, allow corruption and oppression to be woven into our systems and our lives.

Our avoidance of these difficult topics is not unjustified. For we have a long history of dysfunction at the intersection of religion and politics. However, the solution is not to refuse to think or talk about these critical issues. Nor is it to put each issue into a silo and adhere to a hyper-personalized religion and a hyper de-personalized politics. The two are inseparable and intimately affect all of us. If you breathe, you are participating in political life. If you drive, walk on a sidewalk, go to a grocery store, take your children to school, or go to work, you are participating in political life. If you turn on the tap and pour a glass of water or head to the bathroom to take care of your biological necessities, you are participating in political life. Further, if you are a tax-paying person living in America, you are supporting American policy locally, nationally, and internationally with your tax dollars. Whether you agree with these policies or not, you are paying for them. Since we care about our lives, the lives of our families, and even strangers, we must have a say in how our political policies are shaped and implemented.

How? Instead of ignoring these profound truths, we can develop the skills, knowledge, reflection, and practices to enter spaces and conversations about religion and politics rooted in our own beliefs. We can be humble and listen with genuine curiosity, compassion, and a commitment to building communities with room for multiple ways of believing and living. We experience growth when we put ourselves in spaces with people where we confront and wade through the big and challenging questions. We can strike a balance between personal freedom of belief and practice and shared laws that navigate the inevitable points of conflict with awareness, sensitivity, and commitment to justice. Learning our history and understanding our current context helps us build systems that are rooted in shared values, systems that embody daily loving and just policies of living together.

Questions for Reflection

1. What is your understanding of "religious freedom" and "separation of church and state"?

2. How has your faith tradition spoken about and acted on engagement in political life?

3. How does your religion inform your politics? How do your politics inform your faith?

4. What does it mean to "bring your full self" to the world of pluralism, religious freedom, and being an engaged citizen?

3

Rootbound: Taking Time to Think

In the warm summer of 2001, I slept in the basement to keep cool and ward off nausea. I was three months pregnant with my first baby and teaching nutrition classes in the community to people who were receiving food stamps. Each day I drove my old light blue Nissan Sentra around the state with my coworker and friend Selina in the passenger seat. We shared our life stories, listened to music, and laughed as we drove from town to town around northern Colorado teaching nutrition classes in halfway houses, prisons, schools, senior centers, and community centers. I taught in English and she taught in Spanish, and we became fast friends.

A year into our work together I found out I was pregnant, and two months later she found out she was pregnant. We loved sharing the experiences of each stage of pregnancy. When I ran by her desk to tell her I was sick and was heading to the bathroom, she would fill in for me. If she needed an extra hour of sleep in the morning to wait for nausea to fade, I would cover for her. We passed on clothes—I grew out of them just as she was growing into them. She threw me a baby shower, and I threw one for her. When the time came, my baby girl was born, and Selina celebrated with me, brought dinner, and held my baby to her belly, where her baby boy was still growing.

Four days before her due date, Selina called me while I was driving home from visiting my mom with my new baby daughter. Her voice was so serious, I immediately pulled over to the side of the road. I remember the quiet, and the calm, matter-of-fact way she told me that because she hadn't felt her baby move in twenty-four hours, she had decided to go to the midwife we shared. The midwife searched for the heartbeat, but found none. The midwife sent Selina to the hospital where a nurse did an ultrasound. The baby had died; no one knew why. Four days before her due date she was now headed to the hospital to deliver a baby to whom she would then have to say goodbye. I was speechless. There are no words in such moments. When we ended our call, I climbed into the back of my car, unlatched my baby girl from her car seat, held her close, and cried. My head started spinning. How could this happen? Why her? Why will I get to raise my baby and Selina won't get to raise hers?

She delivered the baby, cold and stiff. She held him, dressed him, and named him. The hospital supported her and gave her quiet space to spend hours in the hospital room crying and grieving and letting go. When she got home, I went to visit. Her milk was coming in, but there was no baby to feed. She had to wrap her breasts tight to signal her body to stop producing food for a baby who would never eat. She had to heal from delivery, just as I had so recently done, but she had no baby in her arms to make it all bearable. I remember sitting on her couch, awkwardly. I was young and had never seen such pain up close. I didn't know what to say, so I said the only thing I knew...a statement loaded with bad theology and unexamined assumptions: "Everything happens for a reason." These are not the words a mother wants to hear when she has just lost her baby. What Selina said next rocked my world in all of the best ways. She said, "My priest said this is *not* what God wants. God did not want my baby to die. But it happened." I sat silent, but I ruminated on the words for the days and weeks that followed. How could these two things *both* be right?

We had the most beautiful and heartbreaking funeral for Selina's baby boy. The Catholic priest was compassionate and rejected a Pollyanna view of the horrific pain and suffering of the moment. My friend was resilient and graceful. Unfortunately, our friendship would never be the same. With a new baby at home, I stopped driving around the state to teach nutrition classes. Selina returned to work after taking time to heal. She became pregnant again six months later and had a healthy baby boy. Our lives went on, and my love and gratitude for her is a memory. The questions and the proximity to the pain I felt at that moment became formative in my growing understanding of who I was, who God is, and how we are called to move through the world. I am still embarrassed that I uttered those words of bad theology. When I hear similar sentiments, I cringe and wonder, *Has that person really thought through the logical consequences of that belief?* As I reflect with grace for my younger self, I recognize that back then I had not yet done the work of developing strong roots that could inform the way I cared for and supported Selina in her time of deepest need.

Why We Need Roots

Just as strong and resilient roots are vital to plants and trees, so too strong and resilient roots provide a foundation for us to enter into the chaotic worlds of faith and politics. Roots are a plant's lifeline. Roots anchor the plant in the soil and transfer minerals and water from the soil into the stem and on into the leaves, where they interact with sunlight to produce sugars, flavors, and energy for the plant. The bigger and healthier the root system, the bigger and more robust the plant. Healthy roots contribute to a healthy ecosystem. When one root system is healthy, all of the plants around it benefit.

For us, developing a healthy root system does not mean that our past is free of trouble or that we have everything figured out. Instead, promoting a healthy root system entails a commitment to ongoing learning, growth, and reflection to be able to discern and communicate what we think and why, and how we seek to live in the world. Healthy roots are developed when we have an intentional ethic for living that has been thought through, tested, and repeatedly adjusted so that we can continue to live out our hopes for ourselves and our community. Unfortunately, we are often afraid to enter challenging or difficult spaces. But if we take the time to reach into our own stories and experiences and to dig into our sacred resources, then we are better rooted in what we believe when we step into spaces that challenge us.

While roots are stabilizing, they are also dynamic. Roots are continually weaving and maneuvering through the soil in search of nutrients and space. Just as roots can be trimmed off, some pieces of what we believe can be trimmed off so that other areas have more space to grow. But that growth won't happen unless we nurture our roots.

In my work, I often say that "interfaith" means being rooted in who we are, in our beliefs and traditions, and in being open to one another. I imagine a tree with deep roots and stretching branches. The first and most crucial step is to expand our roots by taking the time to reflect on who we are, what we believe, and how we want to live. These are not questions that deserve stagnant or immutable answers. At our best, we are in a constant process of becoming. Asking who we are, what we believe, and how we want to move through the world are questions that are continually being formed and shaped by our experiences and constant learning. However, to engage in the holy and chaotic worlds of faith and politics with a posture of love and connection, we must take time to reflect and participate in our own formation.

* * * *

Faith Roots

Growing up, I had a clear sense of what it meant to be a good person. I was raised in a family steeped in Christian culture, but who did not go to church regularly. My parents met when they were seventeen years old at a little church in the desert of New River, Arizona, where my great-grandparents had homesteaded fifty years earlier. As for them, for me Christian faith was deeply entwined with the rugged individualism of the Wild West. I learned core values that included moral righteousness, treating one another with care and respect, looking out for those in our community, and helping when someone is in need. I learned a real sense of grace, freedom, and unconditional love from my parents and family. I knew I was loved and saw love shared with those around me. I also grew up with skepticism for institutional religion and a feeling that Christian dogma had brought harm, judgment, and hypocrisy. I was not handed rigid answers to the big questions, nor was I provided with space to reflect critically on how my beliefs have shaped the way I lived. I grew up in a very monolithic white, Christian community with white Christian neighbors and white Christian teachers. My understanding of myself, God, and the world around me was superficial and easily uprooted. I had never been challenged in a way that would invite more deep-seated reflection on the interpersonal or systemic realities around me.

In my mid-twenties, weeks after having our first baby, and around the same time I would grieve with my friend Selina who had lost her baby, my husband and I decided it would be an excellent time to find space to explore and experience a religious community. Driving home from the hospital, we saw the sign for the church where we had done our pre-marital counseling five years earlier, Heart of the Rockies Christian Church (Disciples of Christ) in Fort Collins, Colorado. We decided that the following Sunday would be an excellent time to visit. We knew what we didn't want in a religious community, but we were not exactly sure what else was possible. On our first Sunday, a woman who was not the pastor but a lay member of the congregation was preaching a sermon titled, "Who is God?" My husband and I looked at each other with gratitude as if to say, *You can ask that here?* We liked the place already. In this community, we would find a place to ask big questions. We would find a place to process the complicated and messy worlds of relationships and parenting and explore what it meant to test and live new ideas.

Shortly after beginning to attend services weekly, we approached the pastor to let him know that we would like to read the Bible since we had never really done so (even though I had six of them), and we would like to read it with a group. We offered to host a group weekly in our home if he would provide a list of everyone in their twenties and if he would join us once a month to let us pepper him with questions. I now realize this is every pastor's dream.

Within twenty-four hours, he had given us a list of people. A few weeks later, we had a group of twelve young people gathered in our living room committed to reading the entire Bible together over the course of a year. With our baby sleeping upstairs, we gathered on the couches laughing, eating chips and salsa, and wading through the wild words and worlds of the Bible. Pastor Jeff came once a month and listened to us wondering aloud together as we strove to understand what the biblical stories of concubines, violence and destruction, lepers, and walking on water could possibly mean in the world today.

One year turned into three, and the twelve of us moved through life together. We graduated from the Bible to a Catholic worker social justice series that included reading the Bible as well as classic social justice texts. We gathered for retreats and shared in service projects and processed it all together. Babies were born, jobs were lost, new careers were pursued, and illnesses were faced together. We supported one another, cried together, and celebrated together as we were formed in the Christian faith.

During these five years, I started to step into spaces that were more challenging to me and to work in the community to process and integrate what I was experiencing in our Bible study group. Developing roots is an intentional act of pushing ourselves into new spaces. It requires reframing the beliefs and assumptions we hold dear. I began to teach Sunday School (I learned *far* more than the kids), took a job starting a new non-profit out of the church to support foster and adoptive families, gave birth to a second baby girl, and traveled with the high school group on mission trips. As I began to feel more and more rooted, I began to take more significant opportunities to move outside my comfort zone.

In 2006, my husband and I decided to spend the one week of the year we had away from our two young children (who were spending time with grandparents) volunteering in Boca Chica, a small beach town in the Dominican Republic. Boca Chica is home to Caminante, a program to prevent kids from becoming trapped in the worlds of drugs and child sex trafficking that plague the community. Basking in the newfound learning and growth we were experiencing in our community in Colorado, we had noble intentions in reaching out to our Global Ministries partners, but we had no real idea what we were getting into. When we stepped off the plane into the humid air and tight chaotic airport, we saw a young woman holding a sign that read "Kyle y Amanda." We looked at her with anticipation, hoping she would ease our fears. Her first words were *"Hablas Espanol?"* Our first words were, "No. Do you speak English?" We then sat in awkward silence for the hour drive to Boca Chica in the back of an old maroon Toyota Corolla.

After a slow and emotionally painful ride, we arrived at the housing our mission partners had arranged for us. We walked down the busy alley, past tables of old men sitting on plastic chairs around folding tables where they played dominos, before coming to a flight of stairs secured with an iron gate. We unlocked the gate and walked into a roomy apartment with tile floors, standing water spilling out of the bathroom, no screens in the barred windows, and a basket of fresh fruit on the counter. The apartment was situated across from the dance club whose constant beat shaped the rhythm of our days—and nights. Each morning we walked past food carts, crowing roosters, and morning laughter to the offices of Caminante, where sleeping kids lay spread-eagled on the floor after spending the night in safety. We climbed on the old school bus with more than forty kids who enthusiastically tested their English. We drove thirty minutes past shanties and villages to reach the old school that served as the camp. We navigated the days with our *"muy poco Espanol,"* helping make crafts and stir giant vats of lemonade to serve in small aluminum cups. My husband played a little baseball and wowed the kids with his home run hit, and I pushed little ones on the swings. We met incredible people working to assure a stable future for the kids in their community and were received with hospitality again and again when we most certainly should have been sent home immediately upon realizing we would be far more trouble than help.

The experience provided a space to work through some of the complicated questions I was asking at the time, thanks to the learning and studying we were doing back home. By witnessing the lives of those affected by generations of exploitation, I finally started to recognize the lasting impacts of colonialism and slavery in the Caribbean, specifically in Haiti and the Dominican Republic. I felt the shameful discomfort of my privileged white assumption that I could "go there" and do anything even remotely helpful. I wondered why we had thought it necessary to travel to a different country rather than spend our time and resources closer to home in a community where we could build lasting relationships. I noticed the vast economic disparities and police corruption as we moved through the streets, and wondered how this happens and whether it also happens in my own country. We shared meals in family homes, experienced overwhelming hospitality and kindness, and witnessed resilience and joy as the ultimate forms of resistance.

The experience wasn't perfect by any stretch of the imagination. In many ways, it was a hot mess. But it was formative. I strengthened my commitment to excavating social and political questions, and we had an opportunity to make connections and experience genuine love and compassion. Ultimately, this experience would lead to many other opportunities to move into uncomfortable spaces, to learn, grow, and weave new connections. However, after this experience I worked to be more educated and prepared!

The questions stirring in me after this opportunity only became more complicated after we adopted our son from the Philippines a year later. We made the decision to adopt knowing that we had more love to give and believing that we were up for the inevitable challenges. We intentionally adopted from a country known for ethical practices in adoption. Yet while international adoption is an experience of connection and love, it is also a profound experience of global inequality and human brokenness. The best option is always for a child to have the opportunity to be raised in the culture and family of their birth. Sometimes circumstances make that impossible. My grief for this reality is felt in my body and in our family.

As I already mentioned, my first year as an adoptive mother was both a tremendous gift and one of the most challenging and growth-inducing years of my life. I felt incredible guilt both for having the opportunity to raise a child that had lost the chance to be raised by his birth mother, and for feeling like an imperfect mother. Simultaneously I was mothering two other young children whom I had birthed, and I was struggling to hold it all together. The experiences of adopting and mothering challenged me in ways I had not expected, and led to a deep desire to keep learning and understanding the brokenness I was feeling, and the brokenness of the world. I began to read voraciously in an effort to understand how our beliefs shape our actions, how our actions shape our lives together, and how our experiences together shape our communities and countries. My roots were tested and strengthened as I learned in my body more about loving, and failing, and loving still.

Two years later, I knew I had become rootbound. The container in which I was growing had become constricting; I needed new opportunities to continue learning and growing and to strengthen our connections as a family. After a year of difficult discernment with our family, friends, and pastors, I decided I needed to go to seminary to explore the more significant questions I was longing to understand. We eventually made the decision to sell our home, leave our community, and re-pot our family of five from Colorado to Texas so I could attend seminary and pursue a master's degree in divinity.

When we arrived in Fort Worth, I was immediately smitten. I made my way to campus for the first time, back to school after ten years away, and sat down in a small classroom with one big conference table and nine people from all walks of life circled around. My first class was taught by a big man with rainbow suspenders, a beard, and a thick southern accent. I don't remember what we talked about that day, but I do remember my body being filled with the fire of curiosity. I loved seminary. I loved digging deeper and having time and space to deconstruct and reconstruct my view of God and the world and what it means to live together. I learned about post-colonial theory and womanist theology and liberation theology, and came to see things I did not know I did not know. I studied philosophers and theologians and gained a contextual understanding of the Bible. Each of these learnings helped me to understand better the experiences I had had in places with vast inequality and exploitation. I learned how to listen for voices that had previously been silenced in my life. The new container for my learning was quickly filling with fresh, stronger, and more resilient roots.

While all of the experiences I gained through seminary were transformational, it was my interfaith experiences that proved most formative in helping me discern and articulate what I believed and how I hoped to move through the world. In my second year of seminary, I attended an interfaith seminarians' retreat in the foothills of Texas surrounded by beautiful trees and families of deer. Seminarians gathered in rustic cabins with twenty people from across the country who were studying to become clergy in our respective traditions. Some people there were studying to become priests or pastors, rabbis, or imams. Each of us felt connected and committed in our own culture and were curious to have a relationship with and understanding about people from traditions that weren't our own. About halfway through our time together, it struck me: I was learning as much or more about what *I* believed as I was about what *others* believed and practiced.

Gathered with four others in the living room of a cabin, each of us seminarians shared what we most appreciated about our particular religious tradition. I named how important the practice of communion was to me, and named that in my tradition all are welcome to take and even to serve communion. At this point, the Jewish woman in a chair across from me shared that as a Jewish person, when she is offered communion, she sees it as a sign that a person does not understand or respect her. I was shocked. What I thought was an ultimate sign of welcome and inclusion was to her the exact opposite. She went on to share that for her, as a Jewish woman, to take communion in a Christian church would be a breach of the Jewish identity that she holds dear. Being offered communion means the person offering has not taken the time to understand or care about her Jewish identity.

This encounter challenged my assumptions and helped me to understand and appreciate my own sister's choice not to take communion in my (Protestant) church, as she is a practicing Catholic. Her decision is not a rejection of me; it is an honoring of what is essential to her. As an act of support and love, it is better for me to see how vital her tradition and beliefs are to her than continually to ask her to agree with mine. It is an act of love to seek to understand another person. Perhaps this is an aspect of my ongoing curiosity to learn about the variety of religious beliefs and practices. When we meet people from different religious backgrounds, we can ask how they want to be greeted. We can find out whether they're going to shake hands or simply bow in acknowledgment of the other. Before reaching out to meet or while planning an event, we can check the calendar to make sure that day isn't a holiday in their tradition. If it is a holiday, we can research how to greet them in acknowledgment of the holiday.

Each of these experiences came to shape my religious and spiritual beliefs, as well as my understanding of how to love people in ways that actually feel loving to them. Each time my assumptions are challenged, or I step into a new space of learning and growth, or I move into places closer to pain, my roots deepen and extend further. Shaped by my Christian faith, my experiences with others, and writings of those who have come before me, my roots wind and turn through deeper and deeper soil.

I don't believe it is necessary for everyone to go to seminary to experience this level of faith reflection, but I do think it is beneficial to create the space to reflect and learn as we build a more solid foundation from which to negotiate the big questions of life.

My Roots on Religious Issues:

1. Seek first to understand, then to listen, to ask questions, to think, to pay attention to my body and to what I experience as the Spirit.

2. Know that developing roots is an intentional act of pushing myself into new spaces that will require that I reframe the beliefs and assumptions I hold dear.

3. Love people in ways that actually feel loving to them.

4. Watch and listen for what I do not know. Ask whose voice or experience is silenced or marginalized, and consider how I can better hear those voices.

5. Seek relationships that are mutual, generative, and justice-oriented in every facet of life (partner, family, work, neighbors, community).

6. Hold grace for myself and others in the knowledge that we are all learning.

7. Try again, and never let failure or embarrassment prevent continued learning and living.

Ask yourself:

*   What do I believe?

*   What are the sources that inform my response to this question of belief?

*   Who has shaped me and the lenses through which I view the world?

- Where are my blind spots? What am I missing?

- Whose viewpoint and experience are so far outside of my own that I can hardly fathom them?

- How do my beliefs shape how I relate to those closest to me?

- How do my beliefs shape how I interact with strangers?

- How do my beliefs shape the work I do, the way I parent, and the way I care for my parents?

- How do my beliefs shape the ways I drive, shop, decide where to eat, and choose what to buy?

Political Roots

I mentioned at the outset that my family is Republican. They loved Ronald Reagan and despised Bill Clinton. They disdained taxes and felt that the government should be less involved in our lives. I think my first vote was for Bob Dole, but I honestly don't fully remember. Growing up in north Colorado Springs, everyone was Republican as far as I knew. I think it was not until after college that I met someone who talked about politics from the perspective of a Democrat. The first time I remember thinking critically about politics was in heated conversations over lunch in the sterile yet lively break room at my first job. Just after the 2000 election, there were strong feelings about hanging chads, the Supreme Court, and a stolen election. I naively mentioned that I had voted for Bush because I simply didn't like Al Gore. My dislike wasn't for any particular reason and was not based on any policy or political ideology. I just didn't like him.

In response to this confession, my older and wiser colleague—a good East Coast liberal with dark curly hair and a classic mustache—challenged me. He began to ask my opinion on caring for the poor. He asked what I thought of public education, and corporations receiving outsized tax benefits, and about the very government-funded nutrition programs for which I was working—the Food Stamp Program and the Women Infant and Children nutrition programs. We discussed his opinion that the military exploited those who were poor and people of color and let those with the means avoid service and life risk. As the child of a parent who served in the military and used the GI Bill, this hit close to home. I pushed back and shared how my family had benefited from military service. He pushed back and asked if it was fair that the only way to a college education for so many people of color and people in poverty is to risk their lives in war. For the first time in my adult life, I was being questioned about what I believed politically and challenged to name why. I pushed back and engaged in a thoughtful conversation on politics. My colleague challenged me to think through the repercussions of my vote and invited me to explore the inconsistencies in what I believed and how I participated in public life. It was hard. It was exhilarating.

This conversation coincided more or less with the attacks of September 11, 2001, with my becoming a mother and beginning to attend church, with my reading social justice texts, and with my stepping into spaces with people who were living the repercussions of broken political policies. As a nutritionist, I participated in the annual gathering of the American Dietetic Association and moved through the exhibit halls with a newly forming critical lens. As I passed by lecture hall after lecture hall with scientific and policy presentations sponsored by the Beef Council and the Dairy Council and the Sugar Council, or attended the luncheon sponsored by McDonald's, I began to notice the ways in which the food and restaurant industries shaped the very guidelines I was teaching to those most vulnerable. I started to feel discomfort with ethical inconsistencies, though I did not have the language or framework to know how to communicate my feelings. By the time of the presidential elections of 2004, I was beginning to form political opinions that were more informed and thought through.

By reading and entering spaces where I witnessed inequality, poverty, historical pain, and neglect, I began to ask more critical questions about the invisible systems that shape our lives. Forming my roots meant becoming informed in areas of history and politics and geopolitical power dynamics. For me, this entailed reading and being in conversation with those closest to the brokenness. As I learned, I became more and more comfortable speaking and acting on my beliefs. By the time the 2008 election rolled around, I was all in. I had never experienced a political leader who stood for the policies I hoped would address the inequality and systemic brokenness I had witnessed, and who did so with a way of being that emitted kindness, compassion, and joy. I bought the t-shirts, stuck a sign in my yard, attended the rallies, and canvassed for the new political leader who captured my imagination: Barack Obama.

While my husband and I both felt unabashed enthusiasm for Barack Obama, most members of our families did not. For the first time in my life, I vocally broke with family on something that felt important. While for me this was our way of becoming more aligned with our values and experience of the world, for some of them it felt like a rejection of who they were and how we had been raised. This would be the beginning of many years of navigating political division in our families. Becoming rooted in my political views meant both learning how to stand up for what I believed and learning to embody kindness in the face of difference. Being rooted in my own political perspectives required me to have compassion for those who felt my growth was a rejection of them personally rather than an embrace of my experience and viewpoint.

In the years that followed, my political perspectives were being formed through theological education and through my relationships with people who had been silenced and marginalized. And, while my political party affiliation had changed, I did not have a solid framing for the core principles that guide the way I engage in political work or dialogue. It wasn't until I moved into my work with the Interfaith Alliance of Colorado, stepped into the halls of the legislature, and became privy to behind-the-scenes strategizing and policy making that I developed stronger rooting in how I approach political issues and spaces.

When I first learned about the possibility of working with an organization that stood at the intersection of interfaith work and legislative advocacy, I was ecstatic. My dream job was to do work to build relationships across religious differences and stand up for issues I cared about deeply. However, I knew nothing about political advocacy. I had seen *Schoolhouse Rock!* videos as a kid and had walked through the Colorado State Capitol on a tour. I had knocked on doors for Obama and always voted, but that was the extent of my experience in political advocacy. I shared with the team interviewing me that this would be my most significant learning curve, but that I was excited to learn. They decided to take a chance and committed to showing me the ropes.

On my first time making my way through security at the entry in the basement of the Colorado State Capitol, I was filled with nervous apprehension. On my way to observe the opening of the legislative session, I was unsure of how the whole thing worked. I was still surprised that the Capitol really is "the people's house," and we can walk right in, walk up the intimidating white marble stairs, look up to the inside of the gold dome, and walk right into the chambers. I observed people in suits rushing from one place to the next, hugging and saying hello like long friends who have reconnected after being away. Although there were clear lines of power and differing positions, I was struck by how normal everyone seemed. The people working in our government, making decisions that will shape the lives of millions of people, are just people.

I began attending hearings and committee meetings to experience both sides of a bill being argued. I sat in on stakeholder meetings and testified for the first time in front of a row of legislators on the bill for or against which I was fighting. I remember early on realizing that this was important and incredibly simple. Whereas we tend to regard our democratic process as untouchable or foreign, the truth is that we are our government and our government is us.

As I came to know individual legislators, I realized they each have a worldview and a life of experience that shapes the decisions they make, which in turn shape our lives. I witnessed how we become locked into a position because of our power or party affiliation without thinking through the full details. I also saw the strategies that are behind efforts to hold this power, for better or worse. My observations and learning in my first year working in the Colorado legislature provided political rooting I had never before had. This rooting was less about political party or ideology and more about solidarity, relationship, and commitment to assuring that the core principles in which I believe are woven into the systems that shape our daily lives.

As my political roots continue to grow, I ask: What are my core principles? How do I navigate complex political decisions that pit one value against another within my own value set? Do I follow my political view with purity or with pragmatism? Why? Who suffers when compromises are made? Who suffers if my side loses because we refuse to bend?

In the years leading up to the 2016 election, I observed as much tension within progressive movements as I did between liberal and conservative ones. In fact, arguments within the progressive movements in which I work were at times quite destructive as people acted counter to the core values for which they were fighting. Navigating spaces of contention within groups and between groups requires that we think through what we believe and why, and how we will navigate challenges that inevitably appear.

Ultimately, it's likely that our political views will shift and grow throughout our lives. Muhammad Ali famously said that if a man looks at the world the same way at 50 as he did at 20, he has wasted 30 years of his life. At our best, we will continue to grow and learn through our experiences. Central to this growth is taking time to stop and reflect on what we think and why. When we learn more about how to engage in political issues, we begin to ask about the repercussions of our beliefs, actions, and votes. We can work to find greater alignment between our views about God, caring for our neighbors, and the policies that shape our lives. When we get into the weeds, we soon learn that reality is more complicated than talking points or assumed religious or political alliances. Healthy roots develop when we have an intentional ethic for living that has been thought through, tested, and adjusted as needed. By strengthening our religious and political rooting, we can continue to live out our hopes for ourselves and our communities.

Entering the holy and chaotic spaces of faith and politics means taking the time to know who we are and what we believe, and cultivating practices that will continue to build and nurture our root system. By strengthening our own root system, we are contributing to a healthy ecosystem.

My Roots on Political Issues

1. Seek first to understand. Take in multiple views, and learn the history and context of any particular matter.

2. Ask: Who holds power in this situation? Who benefits from the status quo? Who benefits from change?

3. Ask: What would my silence ensure? What might my voice do to create change?

4. Develop real relationships. Get to know the people who are affected by a political issue, and get to know people holding positions in power. Learn what motivates them and what they care about.

5. Never demonize or dismiss those with opposing political views. I should have a clear argument that states my opinion—and live my view through my actions. This speaks louder than any demonizing can ever do.

6. Hold grace for myself and others. We are all learning.

Questions for Reflection

1. What formative experience significantly shaped the way you view and move through the world?

2. What are the core principles that root you?

3. How have your beliefs on the most critical issues been shaped?

4. Identify a change you have experienced in a core value or belief you held. What prompted that change?

5. What do you experience in your body when you or others confront divisive issues?

4

"I Can't Breathe": Seeing Fear

On a brisk December morning in 2014, I gathered with others outside the Colorado State Capitol for what would be my first protest. The first ruling had just come from a grand jury that there would be no indictment in the killing of Eric Garner in New York City. Along with millions of others, I had watched the video of police putting Eric Garner, a forty-three-year-old black father of six and grandfather of three in a chokehold for more than fifteen seconds for selling individual cigarettes. After releasing the chokehold, the officer pushed his face into the ground. Four officers restrained him as he repeated "I can't breathe" eleven times until he lost consciousness. Waiting for an ambulance, no medical resuscitation or care was given for seven minutes, and Eric Garner died one hour later.

Video of the incident brought to the broader public eye what people in black and brown communities have been experiencing for generations. This horrific event was felt alongside the killings of Trayvon Martin, Michael Brown, Sandra Bland, and others. The series of murders, many of them caught on video, brought to consciousness a reality many in White America had not fully realized: that racism in the U.S. did not end with the Civil Rights movement. It evolved.

Some of the most deeply entrenched racism and sanctioned violence against black people is in our policing and criminal justice systems. Events of the following years continued to shift consciousness for many white folks and call on those of us who were ignorant of and benefiting from the profound racial disparity and violence in our midst to wake up and take action personally to challenge our broken systems. These years prompted in many people a new level of learning and dialogue and called for repentance and transformation of those who had enjoyed a privileged experience that had shielded us from the starkness of these truths in the past.

On this day, I woke up early to drive nervously to the Capitol and join my friends who were leading the Black Lives Matter movement in Denver. I had watched rallies across the country that at times had turned into riots. I had seen people arrested and tear gassed on TV, but I had never experienced those things in person. I did not expect this early morning protest to turn ugly, but these images were stirring in my mind as I took my first baby step into the world of activism. Many of my friends in the Denver Black Lives Matter 5280 chapter were young black academics, pastors, or community leaders, and we were all learning together. Some had grown up assuming that the *worst* racism was in the past. Others had experienced the trauma of growing up amid discrimination and violence. Some had grown up with a *Cosby Show* ideal that told them they could be anything and do anything, but now they watched videos of people who looked like them being shot and killed for the most minor perceived violation of any law—or simply for existing. These images were visceral and emotional for my black friends in ways they could not be for me, and too often my black friends were left having to explain this to white friends. At this moment, we were all navigating new territory and doing our best to figure out a path forward.

On this day, led by the just-forming Black Lives Matter chapter, about forty of us came with a clear list of asks we sought to deliver to the Governor's office. We intended to walk silently into the Colorado State Capitol and say "I can't breathe" eleven times before lying down on the floor of the main gallery for the seven minutes Eric Garner endured without care. It would be a peaceful protest, and we had no intention of taking any harmful or destructive action. We were joined by clergy, community leaders, a few teenagers, and older folks who had been speaking the truth for decades. We made an effort to talk with the Capitol security and even offered them coffee when they came to find out what was happening. However, we soon learned that out of fear they had called for an emergency lockdown of the Capitol, a public building that is typically open all day. The official declaration of a lockdown meant that they could refuse to allow us in. To no avail we calmly spoke with the officers in charge, attempting to assuage their fears. We decided to encircle the building singing traditional songs of liberation until we could meet with the governor or some of our local policy makers. After an hour of singing, and after they realized we would not be giving up, we received an invitation for eight people to meet with the lieutenant governor in his office to go through our requests. I was invited to be one of the small group to walk into the Capitol.

Eight of us joined arms and walked around the building and up the Capitol's back steps to wait outside the large glass door while security gathered to make their plan before permitting us to enter the gates. The eight of us huddled and established our plan: We would hand the lieutenant governor our list and engage in a conversation with him about what the state could do to assure the safety of those in our communities of color in the face of police violence and discrimination. When we finally walked through the doors one by one, we were greeted by nearly thirty officers watching each of us intently. We passed through, putting our phones and bags through the X-ray machine. As I walked through the metal detector, I locked eyes with the officers closely watching me. I was suddenly struck by the scene: All of the Capitol police officers were white, most of them were men, and many of them looked afraid. The fear on the face of one particular young Capitol security officer struck me as I realized that *he was actually scared of us. Little us.* We were a small group of eight. Four of us were clergy wearing collars or stoles. There was a fifteen-year-old boy and his mother, my friend Angela who was a therapist at a residential home for youth, and a young black man who was in the final stage of completing his Ph.D. dissertation in religion. Because of *us,* they had brought thirty police officers to block us from entering the public space of the State Capitol at 8:00 a.m. on a Tuesday.

We eventually sat down inside the lieutenant governor's office and had a poignant conversation. He was a Latino man with a teenage son, and he also felt the gravity of the time. He expressed commitment to using any power he had to work for change in the policing systems. We had conversations about possible ways to improve training and using body cameras, and he listened deeply to the stories of the pain many in the room had experienced. We traded contact information and committed to next steps to open dialogue between community activists, faith leaders, and political leaders to assure police transparency and training. We walked back through the doors, and the officers were all still there. The Capitol was still on lockdown. The fear was thick.

For months I sat with this moment. Of what are we all so afraid? To what has fear driven us? How is fear different for those holding power compared with those who don't?

After the investigation into the shooting of Michael Brown in Ferguson, Missouri, statements reflected how clearly the officer who shot him had created a character in his head. The six-foot-four officer said the six-foot-four Brown made him feel like "a kid holding onto Hulk Hogan." He said he looked like a "demon" charging after him. Michael Brown's family called him "Big Mike." They said he was "funny and good-hearted with an easy smile." Police harassment was a regular part of life for Big Mike and all of the young black men in Ferguson. Their fear and distrust of police officers were profoundly ingrained and reinforced by daily experiences.

I obviously don't know all the details of what happened that fateful day. What I do know is that fear is a powerful force. Fear can change our brain chemistry, affect our nervous system, and build up in our body over time. Fear can shape our decisions and form our habits and patterns of behavior. Fear affects our policies and our laws and shapes the way we vote.

Fear

Much has been said and written about fear. President Franklin Roosevelt famously said, "The only thing we have to fear is fear itself." Author Marianne Williamson is quoted as saying, "Our deepest fear is not that we are inadequate. Our deepest fear is that we are powerful beyond measure. It is our light, not our darkness that most frightens us."[1] Critiques of these quotations will note that they don't account for daily existential physical fear, which is a reality for many around the country and the world. Psychologists have determined that fear is one of a small set of basic human emotions. We can see short-term and long-term effects of the feeling of fear in the brain and in the body. Simultaneously, fear is a vital and enduring evolutionary response that keeps us alive and protect us from real or perceived danger.

We know that there are multiple kinds of fear. Existential fear alerts us to real threats to our physical survival. Rational fears are justified by experiences that confirm the plausibility of our fear being actualized. Irrational fears are less justified or based on plausible realities and can be paralyzing or even lead to psychosis. Fear can protect us from real danger, and fear can inhibit growth and maturity, personally and culturally. Fear can be used as a tool of manipulation or a pathway toward liberation and freedom. I believe there can also be "holy fear" that is rooted in awe, and an invitation into deeper ways of living.

Ultimately, we must build our "fear muscles" to discern and navigate fear if we are to engage in the work of stepping into spaces of religion, politics, and building connections across our differences. These are topics and areas of life that are full of fear-inducing possibilities. The more we have built our fear navigation muscles, the more we will be able to move through these spaces, maintaining our own health and well-being and working for the health and well-being of others.

Fear in the Body

The most common fear I feel is for the physical safety and well-being of my children. Life as a parent seems to come with constant low-level fear. It is not debilitating, of course, and I know all of the rational and spiritual arguments against living with this fear, but the truth is that it is always there. From the first moments of leaving the hospital with a tiny and vulnerable newborn, to the years of slowly learning independence, to the teen years when they drive away in their own car to navigate the

---

[1] Marianne Williamson, *A Return to Love: Reflections on the Principles of "A Course in Miracles,"* (New York: Harpercollins, 1992), 190.

big dangerous world on their own, a parent's deepest fear is that their child will be harmed.

Years ago, my husband and I went to an early-summer pool party at a crowded neighborhood pool. We walked through the doors with our three kids in tow before we each saw friends and quickly scattered, chatting, laughing, and hugging. About twenty minutes in, I realized that while I was keeping an eye on the younger ones, I hadn't seen our oldest child for quite a while. She was six at the time. I surveyed the entire area and still did not see her. My heart quickened, and I started to panic. My stomach turned, and the rush of adrenaline flooded my body. I spotted my husband on the other side of the pool and hurried over to see if he had seen her. He hadn't. My mind raced, imagining all of the worst possible scenarios. The two of us divided up the area and began searching. After what felt like an eternity, I walked into the hallway that led to the locker room and found her curled into a ball. She had become lost and wisely decided to sit and wait until we found her. The look of terror on her face, the tears streaming down her cheeks, and the feeling of fear in my own body are forever seared in my memory.

As soon as we feel fear, the amygdala (a small almond-shaped organ in the center of our brains) sends signals to our autonomic nervous system, which then has a wide range of effects. The autonomic nervous system kicks in: Our heart rate increases, our blood pressure goes up, breathing quickens, and stress hormones such as adrenaline and cortisol are released. The blood flows away from the heart and out toward the extremities, preparing the arms and legs for action. This is the physiological response that has helped us survive for millions of years. Today, however, these responses aren't always helpful.

Fear can cause us to act in ways that are irrational or hurtful as the brain slows down to allow the body to prepare for action. The cerebral cortex, the brain's center for reasoning and judgment, becomes impaired when the amygdala senses fear. The ability to think and reason decreases as time goes on, so thinking amid a state of fear can be impaired. When in a state of fear, some people experience feelings of time slowing down, tunnel vision, or fogginess. These dissociative symptoms can make it hard to stay grounded and think logically in a dangerous situation. The eighteenth-century philosopher Edmund Burke noted that, "No passion so effectually robs the mind of all its powers of acting and reasoning as fear."[2]

Fear as a Tool of Oppression

Though fear is a tool of the evolutionary survival of our bodies, since the Industrial Revolution we have become increasingly sheltered from the predators and threats of the natural world. As our fear of physical threats has fallen, other worries have filled the void. Those seeking to control or shape people's actions often do so through fear. Marketing experts, parents, politicians, and religious leaders all know that fear is a powerful motivator. For thousands of years, political ruling classes have understood the power of intentionally invoking fear as a tool of social control. People will, for the most part, believe what they are told in times of crisis, and so government officials, whether their motives are good or evil, capitalize on or completely fabricate the crises.

We have seen this in our political context today as President Donald Trump claims there is an invasion of illegal immigrants coming across the border bringing drugs, crime, and rape. Even as the facts challenge the narrative of fear, some people accept these stories and remain silent as children are held in cages and thousands of people are subjected to inhumane conditions in the name of national security. The President appeals to our fear to convince our country to spend billions of dollars to "build a wall" to keep the "threatening people" out. These "outsiders," he insists, threaten our physical safety and our economic well-being by taking our jobs and draining our tax dollars. Who these outsiders are shifts through time like a fickle wind: Catholics; the Irish, Japanese, or Mexicans; Jews or Muslims. Stoking our fear assures that the interests of the powerful remain secure. To build just communities in which all can thrive means understanding and confronting the fear of "others" that is deeply ingrained in us, is exploited by those in power, and limits freedom and the possibility for mutual liberation.

---

[2]Edmund Burke, *A Philosophical Enquiry into the Origian of Our deas of the Sublime and Beautiful* (London: R. and J. Dodsley in Pall-mall, 1764), available at https://books.google.com/books?id=KYyhiQencWIC&printsec=frontcover &source=gbs_ge_summary_r&cad=0#v=onepage&q&f=false .

The Story of Lion Cub

In a Hindu story passed on in multiple forms is the story of a lion cub brought up with a flock of sheep. He eats grass like a lamb and even bleats like a lamb. One day a lion appears. Along with the sheep, the lion cub starts running for its life. The lion is surprised to see the cub eating grass like a lamb, bleating like a lamb, and running from the lion in fear of its life. Ignoring the rest of the flock, the lion catches hold of the cub and carries it to a nearby lake. Peering into the water, the cub sees its reflection—along with that of the lion. With a roar like a real lion, all its fears vanish.

Fear of God

While the deeper use of the word *fear* in Judaism, Christianity, and Islam is to evoke a sense of awe and "to know one's place in the universe," religious leaders have often propagated fear to control a community's behavior. They have used threats of pain, hell, and abandonment by God to maintain social hierarchies or limit behavior that they deem "sinful." Of course, the exploitation of fear by people in places of religious power should not diminish the simultaneous use of fear to help people live safely, enjoy healthy relationships, and look beyond their own self-interest in daily living.

The seemingly contradictory imperatives to (1) *fear God* and (2) *not be afraid* are in a sense complementary. Holy *fear* or awe is different from the fear that debilitates and paralyzes and keeps us from being in relationship with one another.

Jewish scholars name that there are two types of fear: lower fear, or fear of punishment; and higher fear, or divine awe. Fear can be seen in religious texts across the Abrahamic faiths as a path to wisdom and maturity. In Christianity, Jesus reminds us that God cares for the birds of the air and God is so intimately present in our lives that even the hairs on our heads are counted, "So do not be afraid; you are of more value than many sparrows" (Matthew 10:31).

Roman Catholicism counts fear as one of the seven gifts of the Holy Spirit. Fear should hold an element of calling us into healthy relationships so that we feel an internal sense of fear of harming others through our actions. Islam follows a similar pattern of nuanced use of the word fear that evokes both divine awe and comfort. Buddhism speaks of fear in the context of recognizing and developing an awareness of the feelings of fear without allowing the feeling to paralyze or inhibit living in peace and improving personal and social well-being. In Buddhism, fear, like other feelings, emotions, and impulses, simply *is*. Our task is to see it, recognize it, and develop the wisdom to be able to discern and let go, to not be controlled by fear. Hinduism teaches that at a philosophical level, fear arises from an awareness that the object of fear is *different* from the subject fearing it. As we grow in wisdom and discernment, we can see what attachment lies at the root of our fear.

Mudras are symbolic hand gestures used in Hindu and Buddhist ceremonies. *Abhaya* (or "fearlessness") is a mudra symbolizing protection, peace, and the dispelling of fear. The gesture is made with the right hand raised to shoulder height, the arm crooked, the palm of the hand facing outward, and the fingers upright and joined. The left hand hangs down at the side of the body. It is nearly always used in images showing the Buddha upright, either immobile with the feet joined or walking.

This mudra, which initially appears to be a natural gesture, was probably used from prehistoric times as a sign of good intentions—the hand raised and unarmed proposes friendship or at least peace. Since antiquity it has been an obvious way of showing that you mean no harm because you are clearly not carrying a weapon.

The Buddhist tradition has an interesting legend behind this mudra: Devadatta, a cousin of the Buddha, through jealousy caused a schism among the disciples of Buddha. As Devadatta's pride increased, he attempted to murder the Buddha. One of his schemes involved setting a rampaging elephant loose, right into the Buddha's path. But as the elephant approached him, Buddha displayed the Abhaya mudra, and this immediately calmed the animal. Accordingly, the gesture signifies not only the appeasement of the senses but also the absence of fear.

You can practice the Abhaya mudra by sitting in a relaxed position with your hands in the Abhaya formation, taking deep breaths, and repeating the word *peace.*[3]

Fear and Liberation

Finding wisdom and clarity amid fear can be exhilarating, and ultimately liberating. Historian Arica L. Coleman reminds us that, "Your fear and ignorance does not change my destiny." She recalls the words of author Zora Neale Hurston: "I am not tragically colored, or female. I am born to make manifest the glory of God that is within me. But it's not just *in* me; it's in everyone, even in you. But we must each choose our own path, fear or liberation. You don't need my permission, and I certainly don't need yours. I have chosen to let my own light shine and to liberate my own self."[4]

Finding liberation in the midst of fear means claiming one's identity and well-being as beyond that which anyone can bestow or limit. This deep belonging and claiming of power challenges the concerns that arise from oppression, feelings of scarcity, or anxieties about an uncertain future.

Each time I step out of the places where I feel safe and known into new situations latent with mystery, uncertainty, and vulnerability, I feel a twinge of fear and hesitation. The feelings increase in intensity as I move further and further out of my comfort zone. Buddhist nun Pema Chodron says, "To be fully alive, fully human,

---

[3]From https://www.lotussculpture.com/mudras.html.

[4]Arica Coleman, "Your Deepest Fear," *LA Progressive* (Sept. 13, 2017), https://www.laprogressive.com/powerful-black-woman/.

and completely awake is to be continually thrown out of the nest."[5] As we find ourselves in ever more challenging spaces, we find we are stronger than we think. We find that while fear has been used to oppress far too many for far too long, fear can also be a tool for growth, wisdom, and liberation. As we learn to navigate fear—and as we grow closer to God, ourselves, and one another—we become free.

Holy Chaos

How do we do this? How do we navigate through fear, uncertainty, and chaos toward wisdom? How do we discern which situations to move into and from which to run? After all, such situations can be complex.

Ask yourself: What is "good" (or better) and what is "bad" (or worse) about this situation? What are my hopes, and how is this situation a part of those hopes? From what and toward what am I moving? *Good* is that which brings freedom, connection, mutual relationships. Goodness generates more goodness and moves us to justice and fairness. *Bad* is that which contains us, keeps us from freedom, oppresses, hurts, and creates disconnection and division.

Navigating Fear

Take as an example navigating the decision of whether there should be armed guards in places of worship. After all, in the past several years we have seen mosques, synagogues, gurdwaras, and churches become locations of violence and murder. Guards make some people feel more safe, while others feel further threatened and traumatized when there are weapons in places of worship. How do we negotiate the real desire for safety with the call to welcome the stranger?

In such a situation, begin by recognizing the fear in your body, and pay attention both to your physical responses and to your instincts at the moment. Take a moment to discern: Of what am I afraid? Am I in *real* or *perceived* danger? What kind of threat is there (physical, emotional, relational)? What are the risks and opportunities in this situation?

---

[5]Pema Chodron, *When Things Fall Apart: Heart Advice for Difficult Times* (1968; Boston: Shambhala, 1997), 70.

What are my hopes/goals? What is the best possible outcome? What is the worst possible outcome? Who *benefits* from my fear or inaction at this moment? Who *suffers* from my inaction? What are the risks in my possible responses? If I step into this space of fear will more 'good' be possible, or could more harm be caused?

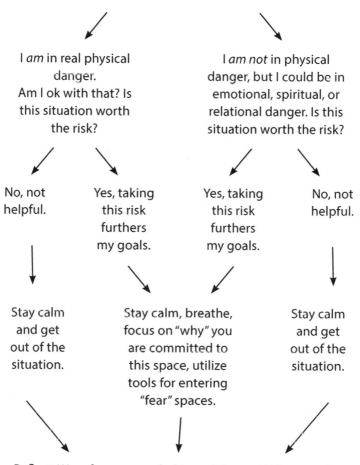

I *am* in real physical danger.
Am I ok with that? Is this situation worth the risk?

I *am not* in physical danger, but I could be in emotional, spiritual, or relational danger. Is this situation worth the risk?

No, not helpful.

Yes, taking this risk furthers my goals.

Yes, taking this risk furthers my goals.

No, not helpful.

Stay calm and get out of the situation.

Stay calm, breathe, focus on "why" you are committed to this space, utilize tools for entering "fear" spaces.

Stay calm and get out of the situation.

Reflect. Were fears grounded in real threats? What was the worst that could have happened? What actually happened? Was anyone hurt by my action or inaction? Was anyone helped? What would I do or say differently? How can I push myself further in healthy ways?

The best way to build resilience in the face of fear is to practice. By doing this in fear-evoking situations, we can develop skills, knowledge, and confidence. Firefighters, public speakers, military officers, doctors, and teachers who expect to experience fear in their daily work train themselves to move through these spaces while controlling their physical and mental fear responses. The more we train ourselves in these spaces, the less likely fear will debilitate us. Just as an athlete trains to build up the ability to run 26.2 miles, or to lift 250 pounds, we can develop our "fear muscles" to enter or be in contentious spaces that are likely to evoke our fear.

So how can we gain better control over our own physiological responses in the face of fear? We begin by teaching our bodies to slow down by slowing down our breathing. If we practice deep, even, controlled breathing when we aren't facing fear-inducing situations, we are more likely to breathe this way when we are faced with a challenge. Slow, even breathing helps to slow down the heart rate and calm the emotions. It can make us feel we are in better control of the situation, and this can help block some of the effects of stress.

Unless we are actually being chased by a bear, we typically have more time than we think to respond to a perceived threat. So step back from a situation and seek clarity before acting. Next, replace fear with curiosity. For fear, particularly irrational fear or fear of "the other," can be grounded in judgments or predictions that may not be accurate or plausible and are often worth a second curious look.

We can shift our mental patterns away from fear and build clarity through embracing a posture of curiosity. Rather than assuming that someone doesn't support LGBTQ people because they are an evangelical Christian, or that they don't believe women should have an equal voice because they are Muslim, we are more able to enter spaces with clarity if we shift from fears and assumptions to wonder and curiosity. "I wonder what their experience with LGBTQ people is?" Or: "I wonder what Islam really says about the role of women?" Moving our mental patterns from fear to curiosity has a profound physical and emotional impact and can reshape relationships as well as the way we see and experience systems and policies.

Muslims in a Maxima

Early on in my time with the Interfaith Alliance of Colorado, I received a call from a man leading a Bible study in Fleming,

Colorado. Though I have lived in Colorado for most of my life and thought I had explored nearly every corner of the state, I had never heard of Fleming, let alone been there. Fleming is a tiny town (population 500) east of Sterling, Colorado, which I had thought was the last stop before Nebraska.

I picked up the phone, and the man on the other end shared that he was leading a weekly Bible study group of about twenty people from a few local congregations. They had been doing a survey of different religions, and at the time they were studying Islam. Over the course of their conversation, they realized that no one in the class had ever actually met a Muslim person. So the leader reached out to me in hopes of learning whether there were any Muslim communities in eastern rural Colorado.

The only Muslim communities I knew of that were remotely close were in the town of Fort Morgan, about an hour away from Fleming. The Muslim community in Fort Morgan is primarily immigrant workers who have come to work in the meatpacking plants. Although I might hope that these communities from Fort Morgan and Fleming would have the opportunity to interact, building that relationship would have been a big leap because the language barrier would not be easily overcome. Instead, I offered to make the two-hour trip east with a group of people who practiced Islam and lived in Denver. The man loved the idea, so I reached out to a few of my Muslim friends to ask if they would be interested in a road trip.

A month later, Ismail, Ismail (yes, two Ismails), and Iman and I climbed into my Nissan Maxima and headed east. In a play on the "Nuns on the Bus" tour for social justice advocacy trope, I called our trip "Muslims in a Maxima." Our time in the car proved to be fun and enlightening. I quickly realized that new experiences would be had not only by those in rural Colorado whom we were going to visit, but also by those of us making the trip.

Iman is a Denver-born child of Palestinian immigrants. She is "American" through and through, and is deeply committed and connected to her family home in Palestine. Both Ismails are of Turkish descent and are part of the Gulen Muslim movement. Each had gone to college in Europe and come to the U.S. to work and raise their children. None of the three had spent much, if any, time in rural America. As we stopped for gas, it became clear that

Iman was enamored by the wide-open fields and the spotted cows sidling up to the fence near the gas pumps. As we continued, we shared stories of our childhoods and the landscapes in which we each felt at home.

Finally, we pulled into Fleming and quickly found the small Church of the Brethren in the row of buildings on the town's Main Street. We made our way into the little church that reminded me of the small Baptist churches to which my grandparents took me as a kid in rural California. We were greeted by a kind and cautious man who let us know there was a lot of buzz in town about our visit. He wasn't sure exactly how many people would be coming, as people from the group had met some resistance from friends and neighbors. At about ten minutes before 2:00 p.m., people started to arrive, bearing potluck dishes to share before the discussion. We slowly gathered in the fellowship space at the back of the sanctuary, and soon the line of folding tables was covered with delicious casserole dishes. Nervous energy pulsed through the room as twenty of us filled plates with food and formed a circle with our chairs.

After sharing a meal and engaging in small talk, we began with introductions. Although everyone was there to hear a presentation from our leaders from the Muslim community, we started by inviting people to share a bit about themselves. We asked everyone to share their name, identify their community, say what had inspired them to come to the gathering, and then tell about something that makes them feel alive. Sharing started slowly, with surface-level niceties, until the third person around the circle named that she was a bit nervous about this gathering. She shared that her neighbors had heard she would be meeting with Muslim people, and that they had warned her that it would be dangerous, but she came anyway. She then told us about her cat who had been sick and about her neighbor who had been helping her care for her cat. The next person told of the checker at the grocery store the day before who had said to her, "I hear Muslims are coming to Fleming." We all laughed at how quickly word had spread that there would be unlikely guests in town. Some people in the group told of how they had moved to the small town for a simpler life, while others spoke of how they had been born and raised there. A mother shared with pride that her son was serving in the Air Force, and another that she was hoping her daughter would move back to Fleming from Denver.

The circle of introductions came around to my friend Iman. With a big smile, she laughed and noted how much she had in common with everyone around the circle. She said that she too had a cat that brought joy to her life and expressed sympathy for the woman whose cat was sick. She named that her brother is an officer in the Air Force serving in Washington, D.C., and shared how proud her parents were of him as well. Her family, specifically the parents for whom she cares and to whom she is committed, she identified as the most essential part of her life. The air in the room lightened, and the eyes of the people around the circle widened. People nodded and laughed and felt a clear connection to Iman—a first-generation Palestinian American Muslim woman raised in the city. The presentations went on, now with Iman, Ismail, and Ismail sharing about the five Pillars of Islam and noting the lines of connection between Islam, Christianity, and Judaism. They shared bits of the cultural nuances between the ways Islam is experienced around the world and noted that Muslim people have been living in the United States since its founding.

However, the most essential thing shared was not information but the human connections that dispelled the fears of each person who had walked into the little white church in Fleming, Colorado, to meet with three Muslims and a Christian pastor who had driven up from the big city in an old Nissan Maxima.

Questions for Reflection

1. What sensations do you have in your body when you feel fear?

2. How do you differentiate between the various kinds of fear?

3. What practices do you employ that build wisdom and resilience in the face of fear?

4. When have you regretted not stepping into a situation because you were afraid?

5. When have you regretted not listening to fear before stepping into a new situation?

5

Embracing Curiosity:
Wonder as an Act of Justice

It was a cold, snowy day in January when I walked into the Colorado History Museum to host a gathering to discuss the intersection of race and religion. In preparation, I had worked with two partners who were black leaders in our community, but scheduling conflicts had come up right at the end, and neither could be there for the actual event. We built the gathering around a compelling exhibit on racism, and invited participants to tour the exhibition and then to gather and break into small groups for conversation about the ways in which religion has perpetuated or challenged racism.

I didn't know how many people to expect; I thought perhaps thirty or forty. I had reached out to about five faith leaders in the community whom I had asked to serve as facilitators of the small groups. I came into the event feeling green, frazzled, overwhelmed, alone, and sorely unprepared for such an important and complex conversation.

So as more and more people walked through the door, I began to panic. More than one hundred people came! Clearly, this was a topic that people were hungry to discuss. People I knew and people I had never met walked through the door expectantly. I took a deep breath, pulled myself together to welcome everyone, and explained how the event had come to be: that we were in a time of deep reflection as a country following the very public deaths of people of color at the hands of police. A hot debate had ensued nationwide that revealed the deep divisions that had long existed but to which many of us had become complacent. Conversations were stirring within religious communities as to how faith communities and religious teachings had perpetuated racism, and we were working to open up this conversation. I noted that religion has long been used both to oppress and to liberate. This has been especially true in the realities of racism.

As people poured in, I realized we were going to need more people than I had anticipated to facilitate the small groups. I identified several additional leaders in the room whom I knew, and pulled them aside to see if they would lead. I set the stage with the large group using guidelines for dialogue I had learned through my work with Parker Palmer's book *Healing the Heart of Democracy.*[1] After our whole-group introduction, everyone spread out into groups of ten. Facilitators reintroduced the guidelines and then began with the provided questions.

As I walked around the room, observing the conversation and dynamics, I saw people engaged in deep thought and dialogue. I noticed groups in which one person was hogging the airspace and made notes of what I would do differently next time.

At the end of the event, I took another deep breath, grateful that the event was over, cleaned up my things, and went home to collapse on my couch for a nap.

A few days later, I received an email from a couple, Harold and Claudia, who had attended the gathering Harold and had led conversations on race in Denver for twenty years. They kindly expressed gratitude for the event and for the intention to open up this meaningful conversation. They went on to name some of the aspects of the event they found concerning. They asked if we might meet in person so they could share from their experience. Although my initial reaction was defensiveness and resistance, I took a breath and embraced gratitude that they had reached out

---

[1] Parker J. Palmer, *Healing the Heart of Democracy: The Courage to Create a Politics Worthy of the Human Spirit* (San Francisco: Jossey-Bass, 2011).

to me and that they were willing to help me learn. I replied to the email, and we set a time to meet the following week.

They walked into my office in an old church, and we found a comfortable place to sit. As we began to talk, I could tell they were both loving and gracious. I could see that they observed my newness and my potential to grow—and the harm I could do if I were not supported in that growth. They expressed kind words about my stepping into this space of essential conversations, and shared about their decades of experience confronting racism. Harold grown up in Tulsa, Oklahoma, where historical pain of race riots of the 1920s lingered in the city. Harold shared about years of writing, thinking, and facilitating education and dialogue around race before naming the ways their experience at the event I had led had been harmful.

They expressed concern about the guidelines I had provided, and they specifically noted the ways in which the instructions perpetuated individualism and discounted the emotional and communal depth of the historical trauma of racism.

They told me there had been a person in their group who had been domineering in ways that were hurtful to the others in the group, perpetuating white supremacy through his actions. They noted that the facilitator of the group was clearly unprepared, inexperienced, and not able to confront the person to bring the group back to the focus, most likely because I had not prepared them adequately. They asked me questions about my hopes and what I was feeling about the event. They concluded our meeting with an invitation to attend one of their monthly gatherings where people discussed topics related to racism, and they handed me a poem written by a black woman who attended their group. She had written the poem for the white folks in the group whom she observed struggling as they came to terms with their role in perpetuating racist systems and structures.

How Does It Feel?

I wonder about you

About all the feelings you don't know you have

About how it feels to wake up to your bondage

When you thought you were free.

Oh, I do wonder

How it feels to realize

You've been in the conversation all along

Only you weren't talking

And had never learned the language.

And I wonder

How does it feel the day you realize

You are afraid to speak of this to your own race

Because you will risk a lifetime's investment

In your own whiteness.

Yes, I wonder about you

About your journey to freedom

About your awakening to feelings

And thoughts and awkwardness

And even why you show up at all.

But just for a moment, I stop wondering

When you stand beside me

Without boasting or justifying

Or taking up all the space

And listen.

Copyright: Norma Johnson, April 17, 2012, Boulder, CO

The poem and the way in which Harold and Claudia reached out to me have become one of the greatest gifts to my learning and growth. They had a definite issue with the way I had led the event. Rather than merely dismissing me, or condemning me, they invited me into a relationship through the lens of curiosity and wonder. They handed me insights from their experience and inspired me to explore my questions more deeply. Through this experience, I continued to learn and read and listen and step into new and challenging relationships.

Subsequently, I learned from the information they provided and asked them if they would partner in building a workshop called "Facing Racism" to be offered to our organizational leaders and to the congregations who partnered with us. This gathering seeded what developed into a series of workshops for people in faith communities to *see* and *confront* the racism that is deeply embedded in our minds and our systems. The program came to life thanks to two black women friends who developed and launched the project to be led in primarily white faith communities.

Simple judgment or ambivalence would have ended the conversation that had started at the event at the history museum that cold day in January. Harold and Claudia easily could have dismissed me as another white person wading into the territory of racism, ignorant and unprepared. From a place of my own defensiveness, fragility, or even exhaustion, I could have rejected the email they sent. Instead, Harold and Claudia were curious enough to learn more about my thinking and my hopes for growth, so they sent an email. I was curious enough about their experiences and the wisdom they could offer me, so I reached out and set up a time for us to meet.

Curiosity has the power to open minds and transform lives. Curiosity is distinctly different from judgment or fear, which both narrow our vision and clench our "truth" in our fist. Curiosity is an open hand reaching out to know more and to be in a relationship. This is the path of real justice and mutual liberation.

* * * *

For better and for worse, I have always been curious. I am not content with simple answers or with accepting the status quo compliantly. Early on, I wondered how my Christian friends could claim that *their way* was the *only way*. What about all of those other people around the world? Growing up surrounded by people who were adamantly sure that their faith was the only true faith, I wondered how we, a tiny group of people on this vast and wild planet in the vast enormity of time and space, could actually *know* the answers? And why would God make the one answer to all things so narrow while also creating this multifarious fascinating world of nature and people? When I asked these questions aloud, I was at times condemned or dismissed. In my world, those who challenged the assumed answers to the big questions were ignored—or worse, condemned—to eternal damnation.

As I grew older and began to meet people from different parts of the world and from different religious traditions, I asked new questions. Rather than being concerned with one right answer (I don't believe that is what life or God is about), I began to wonder how our different understandings of God and religion shape the ways we treat one another. How do our views of God shape the ways we move through the world? How do our views of God inform the ways we determine our laws and shared government? How do our views of God shape our experiences of the geopolitical realities of war and peace? How can we each learn from the many ways we experience God? For me, these are both spiritual and pragmatic questions. How do we find meaning and connection personally and communally, *and* how do we live together through shared laws and policies?

Curious Brains

Embracing curiosity and asking questions involves an inherent assumption that we don't have all of the answers. Embracing curiosity creates space for learning and growth, and practicing curiosity actually changes our brains. A recent study published in *Neuron* magazine suggested that as we become curious, our brain's chemistry changes and in turn helps us to retain information and increase our learning.[2] Researchers found that when monitoring brain activity using an MRI machine, the area of the brain that regulates pleasure and reward lights up when the participants in a study have their curiosity piqued. Additionally, the hippocampus, the area of the brain that is involved in creation of memories, shows increased activity. When we experience both curiosity and the potential of a reward, our body releases dopamine, which gives us a natural high and plays a role in enhancing the connections between cells that are involved in learning. We all know that the best way to break down stereotypes and assumptions is through story and relationship. When we build relationships across differences that pique our

---

[2]Matthias J. Gruber, Bernard D. Gelman, Charan Ranganath, "States of Curiosity Modulate Hippocampus-Dependent Learning via the Dopaminergic Circuit," *Neuron* 84:2 (Oct. 22, 2014), https://www.cell.com/neuron/fulltext/S0896-6273(14)00804-6.

curiosity, we are actually creating new pathways of connection and memory within us and between us.

Todd Kashdan, professor of psychology and senior scientist at the Center for the Advancement of Well-Being at George Mason University, says that curiosity can be defined as the recognition, pursuit, and desire to explore novel, uncertain, complex, and ambiguous events.[3] He names the fact that actually identifying and understanding curiosity has been an elusive pursuit for theorists and psychologists, although there is broad agreement that curiosity is a natural trait critical to human growth and survival. In the long term, acting on one's curiosity functions to expand knowledge, build competence, strengthen social relationships, and increase intellectual and creative capacities. Kashdan has created a scale of five dimensions of curiosity, naming the multiple ways in which curiosity functions to increase joy, build resilience, and support efforts to solve complex problems and navigate stress-inducing situations.[4]

Cultivating curiosity, in its multiple dimensions, is a vital virtue and a necessary skill for seeking justice and engaging ways of connecting across our religious and political differences. Business philosopher Fred Kofman speaks of the difference between *learners* and *knowers*.[5] He begins by observing that we each see the world through different lenses, and that no individual can hold all of the information that is possible to see and capture through the many existent lenses. He notes that we are better able to gain clarity and effectiveness when we work together with people who see through different lenses. Then he observes that *knowers* receive self-worth and identity through being right and holding the complete truth. Knowers regard anyone who disagrees as inferior at best or an enemy at worst because a knower's all-encompassing truth cannot be challenged. The language knowers use expresses beliefs and

[3]Todd B. Kashdan and Paul J. Silvia, "Curiosity and Interest: The Benefits of Thriving on Novelty and Challenge," *The Oxford Handbook of Positive Psychology*, 2d ed., ed. Shane J. Lopez and C. R. Snyder (New York: Oxford Univ. Press, 2011): 367. Available at https://www.researchgate.net/publication/232709031_Curiosity_and_Interest_The_Benefits_of_Thriving_on_Novelty_and_Challenge.

[4]Todd B. Kashdan et al., "The five-dimensional curiosity scale: Capturing the bandwidth of curiosity and indentifying four unique subroups of curious people," *Journal of Research in Personality* 73 (2018): 130–49.

[5]Fred Kofman, *Conscious Business: How to Build Value through Values*, reprint ed. (Boulder, Colo.: Sounds True, 2013).

opinions as indisputable facts without room for humility or growth. We all act as *knowers* at one point or another.

Learners, by contrast, experience self-worth based on the ability to acquire new knowledge and understanding and continuing to grow in effectiveness. Learners realize they hold only one piece of a complete story and spend time listening, gathering further information and insights, and partnering with others with different views to meet shared goals. We all act as learners at one point or another, and the more we can cultivate practices of *learning* and curiosity, the more we can build relationships across our many differences, and the more we can work for progress on our most pressing social issues. Intentionally embracing ways of learning and curiosity is key to transformation.

	Knower	Learner
Values	knowledge and reputation • makes no mistakes • defensive (claims to know how things are or ought to be)	being effective and learning • admits mistakes • not knowing isn't a problem
Self-esteem	is coupled to "being right" • hides doubts • arguing (wants to win)	is coupled to learning • open about doubts • curious (wants to understand other points of view)
Attitude	rather arrogant • opinions are presented as facts	rather humble and/or serving • offers opinions/views as options
Approach	I am what I think • disagreements are personal attacks	I reflect • disagreements are learning opportunities

(Bert Krijnen, ""How Mindsets Make Big Differences: Knower vs. Learner," *Con-TACT* (August 2018), https://www.con-tact-international.com/how-mindsets-make-big-differences/)

Too Much Information, Too Little Curiosity

We have any information we desire at our fingertips or sitting in our pocket. Can't remember the name of the actor who played opposite Tom Cruise in *Top Gun*? Google it. Wondering what the population of Zimbabwe is? Search Wikipedia. We are bombarded by information intentionally designed to capture our attention and tap into our conscious and subconscious desires. Pop-up windows aim to catch our eye and lure us into the rabbit hole of the Internet.

With so much information available, many of us subconsciously close ourselves off to new information. Perhaps it is because we have so much information coming at us that we simply cannot filter what is important and what is not. Perhaps it is because of our lack of ability to deal with things that challenge our current frameworks of reality that we are drawn to information that simply confirms what we already know. We reject any information that challenges our assumptions and affirm information that reinforces our deeply held views. If the information we receive does not align with what we know we know, we declare it to be "fake news." In our personal relationships, our social network circles, and our news outlets we tend to surround ourselves with people who will not challenge what we already know.

Fear and disdain for information that challenges what we know is not new. Curiosity that pushes us to question something deemed to be a truth has been condemned for millennia. Yet actually curiosity comes from a posture of longing to know more. Digging into the big questions reveals gaps in our knowledge and imperfection in our systems. Politicians may resist exploring alternative health care models for fear of disrupting the current system, which benefits insurance company shareholders. The NRA has done everything in its power to prevent even basic research from being conducted on the impact of gun violence on public health. The truth is that curiosity can be a radical and subversive act as we expand our thinking beyond assumptions that maintain the status quo. Curiosity can lead to transformation as we leave old power patterns behind and embrace transformative relationships grounded in continually learning and seeking to understand and care for one another.

Religious Curiosity

In religious circles particularly, curiosity can be seen as a threat to the absolute truth the religion allegedly proclaims. Perhaps you have run across religious people who fear that followers will be led astray if they ask questions or seek experiences outside of their particular community's beliefs and practices. Conservative Christian websites warn parents to remind their children that curiosity can lead to sin and eternal damnation. They point to stories such as that of Eve, whose "curiosity" drove her to eat the fruit of the tree of knowledge of good and evil, banishing people from the Garden of Eden. Or to the story of Lot's wife, who couldn't resist looking back and was turned into a pillar of salt. Stories such as these (notice: both about women trespassing in the name of curiosity) are used to warn of the evils and inevitable downfall that result from asking questions and seeking knowledge. The Christian tradition typically presents doubting Thomas, who asks to see the scars on the hands of Jesus before he will believe his eyes, as less faithful than other disciples. Religious certainty is rewarded as being superior to questions, curiosity, and seeking. The more certain a person is about their faith, the more loyal and dedicated they appear.

Of course, this is not true for every religious tradition, nor is it universally true within Christian scripture or tradition. In Exodus 3:3 we read of Moses' curiously approaching a burning bush, saying to himself, "I must turn aside and look at this great sight, and see why the bush is not burned up." Although often we focus on the story of Abraham's faithfully walking up the mountain to follow God's order to sacrifice his son without question, we can see throughout the relationship between God and Abraham that Abraham is constantly questioning, seeking to know more, trying to challenge God. God is experienced in the space of curiosity and wonder. In the Christian scriptures, we see from the earliest pieces of the story of Jesus that people are curious to know who he is and what his life means. From shepherds to tax collectors, from soldiers to women in need of healing, people curiously approach Jesus to experience the mysterious works they have heard about. In Matthew 7:7, part of the Sermon on the Mount, Jesus says, "Ask, and it will be given you; search, and you will find; knock, and the door will be opened for you." This is not a one-time invitation, but a call continually to seek the ways of God from a posture of humility and "not knowing." For many Christians, this is a call to curiosity, a call to seek to understand God and to deepen understanding of what it means to follow the great commandment, to love God and to love one another.

My rabbi friends remind me that *questioning* is at the heart of Jewish practice. The early Jewish community was based around life in the Temple. After the Temple was destroyed in the first century, Jewish communities had to reorient their lives around a new collective commitment. In the rabbinic period, the unifying force was around education and learning of the Torah, Midrash, and the Talmud. The practice of debate and questioning around meaning and contexts was crystallized into the Talmud. In the debates over meaning, there are no right answers. For each verse analyzed in the Talmud, there are pages of arguments between Jewish thinkers about even the smallest details. Curiosity, question, and debate remain assumed virtues within much of Jewish tradition.

The Buddha is known to have taught patience as a central teaching of the practice toward enlightenment. However, the patience of which the Buddha spoke is not the patience of stagnation, but patience such as that of an artist or a musician working to refine and master a craft. This patience is paired with curiosity as one is invited to seek continuously to know more about the body, the breath, the passing emotion, the underlying pain or suffering, the joy or feelings of fulfillment. The practices of developing mindfulness embody a patient curiosity as we continually move deeper into the breath and the body, recognizing the thoughts and sensations that come alongside us. The Buddha did not provide a precise method or system of meditation and the path to enlightenment. There is room for discovery on the road, led by one's sense of curiosity and discernment.

My experience is that the more I have learned about different religions and the more I have nurtured an insatiable curiosity for the many ways people experience and pass on knowledge about God, the more I have come to understand and appreciate my own Christian tradition. Curiosity drives me to learn more about my own faith, to explore different ways of praying, to learn more about the history and culture of the Bible, and to listen for the ways a person's understanding of Christianity shapes the ways they move through the world. Curiosity about Judaism, Islam, Buddhism, Sikhism, and Hinduism has deepened my own spiritual experience and invited relationships that are full of wonder and joy. Curiosity provides the opportunity to enjoy foods from every continent, to hear music that moves beyond language or culture, and to find human connections I couldn't have imagined. Ultimately, I believe it is these seeds, rooted in curiosity, that grow into ally- and partnerships as we build communities in which all people are treated with dignity and respect.

Politically Curious

Curiosity has not typically been a virtue in political life. Curiosity takes time and embraces a level of uncertainty and change, qualities that are seen as inhibitors to political expediency and continuity of the status quo. Politicians are rewarded for having unchanging and unchallenged views. Curiosity and expressed openness to other viewpoints or experiences can be punished at the polls. People whose views or perspectives change, even if due to new learning or skills, are dubbed wishy-washy or flip-floppers. Even simple conversations "across the aisle" are considered by some people to be betrayals to strident views on any particular topic. In politics, power is king, and power is often bestowed on those who confidently and brazenly fight for *their truth* to win. Precise and efficient outcomes are desired over embarking on somewhat open-ended processes guided by curiosity and openness to new and creative paths forward.

In this light, curiosity can be seen as a countercultural act of justice-seeking. Philosopher Michel Foucault identifies the social function and value of curiosity, namely that curiosity "evokes the care one takes of what exists and what might exist." He observes that our curiosity about the lives of others can be a source of empathy and, in turn, cooperation. Foucault argues that curiosity is not only an under-appreciated method of philosophy but also a critical practice for building inclusive political communities. Curiosity can be a practice that destabilizes and transforms the status quo. Although philosophy has historically dismissed this way of understanding curiosity in favor of a respectful and reliable wonder, curiosity is an invitation to disrupt oppressive systems and imagine new possibilities. At the root of justice is a moral imagination that creates space for new paths forward. We cannot remain entrenched in ways of being that have divided and oppressed; our task is to see beyond what we *know* and to live into habits that will move us toward mutual liberation.

Contemporary political surveys show that people are entrenched ideologically. Only a tiny percentage of people in the middle are open to movement. On the most divisive political issues, people are not moved by facts or statistics. This reality challenges long-held assumptions that education and information are keys to building movements for change. Yet a recent study published in *Advances in Political Psychology* identifies one antidote to politically entrenched ideology: curiosity.[6] The study set out to measure "science curiosity" to create engaging science documentaries. The researchers discovered that curiosity was a critical factor in openness to receiving, processing, and integrating new information. Those who were self-identified as "knowledgeable" were more politically polarized, regardless of facts provided counter to their assumptions. Those who were more "curious" were less politically polarized and more moved by new information.

This was the first study in an emerging field, but one that holds great potential to move us out of our ideologically polarized corners. Can we foster curiosity as a way of being that helps us move beyond partisan politics? Are there ways to help spark curiosity, knowing that curiosity activates pleasure centers in our brains? Might wonder be key to finding consensus and commitment to our shared hopes in a politically polarized country? Might we see curiosity as more than an external source of entertainment, but as actually integral to justice-seeking, integral to religious practice, integral to political imagination, and essential to policy making beyond locked partisan fights?

Cultivating Curiosity

Curiosity is a practice that can be developed intentionally and evoked in our communities. What might it look like to cultivate curiosity in our relationships? How might cultivating curiosity help build partnerships across religious and ideological differences? How

6Dan M. Kahan, Asheley Landrum, Katie Carpenter, Laura Helft, and Kathleen Hall Jamieson, "Science Curiosity and Political Information Processing," *Advances in Political Psychology* 38, vol. S1 (February 2017): 179–99, https://doi.org/10.1111/pops.12396.

might we use curiosity to shift our conversations about politics with those we can't seem to understand?

1. *When the going gets rough, turn to wonder.* Taking a cue from the work of Parker Palmer, this is an invitation to shift our mind to "I wonder..." when we feel judgment creeping in. When someone says something that strikes us as offensive or uninformed, we can ask, "I wonder...what in their experience has led them to feel this way?"

2. *See monotonous situations as opportunities to pay attention.* Whether standing in line at the grocery store, waiting in traffic, or sitting at the DMV, we can take the opportunity to pay attention to the little details and even to turn to the person next to us and ask a question. See every opportunity as a chance to peel back a layer of your assumptions.

3. *Resist fear and try something new.* Push yourself just outside your comfort zone and focus on the possibilities of moving into new spaces. Test out the theory that curiosity activates the pleasure receptors in your brain and step into a unique and challenging situation. Visit a mosque and get to know people in your local Muslim community. Many mosques have regular open house times designed to break down fear in their communities. Enter a space where you expect people with a different political identity will be. Go to a rodeo or an art museum and simply observe and talk to the people around you without judgment.

4. *Dive into something that interests you.* Make time to follow a latent passion. Have you always been curious about learning to play the guitar or planting a garden? By creating space to follow your curiosity and passion, you will develop pathways that will transfer to other areas of life as well.

5. *Read.* It sparks the imagination. Whether fiction or nonfiction, magazines or novels, reading introduces new words, ideas, and stories that engage our sense of curiosity and leave us with questions to explore. Thoughtful reading often takes a backseat to the demands of our days. Yet creating blocks of time to dive into reading can pay off in stronger relationships and a more productive work life—and simple enjoyment.

6. *Slow down and take your time.* One of the biggest obstacles to curiosity is busyness. When we are rushing through the days,

we don't have time to stop to wonder. If necessary, block out time on your calendar to slow down, think, observe, take a slow walk, or have space for more in-depth conversations with people you would like to get to know.

7. *Practice asking "Why?"* Someone once said, "Knowledge is having the right answer. Intelligence is asking the right question." Don't be afraid of looking ignorant by asking questions. Even when you aren't sure you have a question, probe a bit more and find a question. Whether you are seeking a solution to an entrenched problem or simply getting to know someone new, the practice of asking questions helps you explore the multiple layers of each issue or person. One question leads to another. Realizing that *the more you know the more you don't know* is an excellent place to be.

8. *Practice saying less.* According to the ancient Greek philosopher Epictetus, "We have two ears and one mouth so that we can listen twice as much as we speak." The practice of listening without planning what we will say next builds our skills for actually being curious about what others are saying and strengthens our understanding and care of others. It also makes us more enjoyable to be around. It is better to be interest*ed* than interest*ing*.

9. *Hang out with a child.* Slow down and actually *be* with a child by taking a slow nature walk or reading a book. See the world through the child's eyes. Watch their expressions as they try on new emotions and observations about the world around them. Watch the way they express themselves through feelings of joy, confusion, or anger. Respond to their "why?" with your own "why?" by inquiring into their imagination. "Why do *you* think the sky is blue?" Hear what they say with joy and wonder.

10. *Travel somewhere new.* You don't have to spend the money to fly to the jungles of South America or the streets of London—though that would be wonderful too! You can find a neighborhood in your town you have never been to and visit a local coffee shop or grocery store. You can make a road trip to a small town or forest nearby that you have never seen. Go to new places with an open agenda and an open mind

and observe people and landscapes. Follow where your own curiosity leads.

Curiosity can be cultivated. We can actively choose to move through our days with a sense of wonder. This is a radical act of justice-seeking, not merely an indulgent source of entertainment. We can evoke curiosity in others by asking questions and modeling our own ability and desire to know more about them, their lives, and their view of the world. Our words and our posture can move communities from "knowing" to "learning" as we see one another with greater compassion and wonder and as we break down stereotypes and assumptions.

* * * *

When I was nineteen years old, I had the opportunity to spend a month in Singapore, where my dad was working as a computer programmer. It was my first time leaving the U.S., and I had no idea what to expect. I remember the long plane ride, and I was quite taken by the warm towels that the flight attendants on Singapore Airlines gave us before landing. I remember arriving on New Year's Eve and through my jet-lagged stupor watching a firework display from the apartment balcony. I remember the trucks with mobile billboards and blaring propaganda for the upcoming presidential election. Each day I jumped on the bus that stopped outside Dad's apartment and explored the city. I tasted new foods and saw new sights as I meandered through markets. I found running trails and parks and sat on the shore and watched the shipping barges come through the port. Awestruck, I walked through giant malls and observed all of the different people and languages.

One weekend, my dad and I took a ferry across the channel to Malaysia and rode bikes through the Malaysian countryside. The images of the small villages and children remain clear in my mind. We passed little street markets and dozens of cats whose tails had been chopped off to keep them out of the food before we found a local motel to stay the night. We each slept on an old twin bed and used the hole in the ground that served as a toilet. The second day we rode to a magical beach with giant black rocks and tiny smooth, creamy colored shells covering the shore. I seem to remember every detail of that trip, but what stayed with me particularly was a lasting taste for exploration and adventure. I nurtured this passion for travel by taking any chance I could to explore different countries and meet new people.

Years later, in my first year of seminary, I had the opportunity to travel to Israel and Palestine. On this trip I experienced the integration of learning and experiencing a new place. I was deep into Hebrew Bible classes, thinking theologically about everything around me, and had just taken a "Women in Early Christian History" course in which we had learned about the very sites I would be seeing. The tour was led by my pastor from home, and I was overwhelmed to be entering sacred spaces I had heard about since childhood. I was awestruck by the diversity and beauty of the land, with its deserts juxtaposed with lush trees and gardens. The Sea of Galilee felt serene and holy (even with the touristy fish restaurant at the shore). Floating in the Dead Sea covered in mud was an otherworldly experience. The food was phenomenal, and the hospitality was inspiring. But what struck me most was the people— the people who invited us into their homes in Bethlehem, or who told us about their persistent work using music as a tool for peace, or who had lived in refugee camps for generations. We heard stories from Israeli settlers who had moved to Israel from Russia seeking a Jewish homeland, and from Quakers who had lost their Palestinian homes in 1967 and have been working for peace ever since.

The people and the land fed my curious spirit and left me longing to understand more about the conflict that was at the heart of so much pain. I wanted to know more about the history of colonialism that shapes our lives to this day, and about the different religious traditions that sustain, motivate, and often divide people in the Middle East and beyond. Upon returning home, I looked for opportunities to continue this learning. I attended an interfaith seminarians' retreat, as well as an interfaith women's group called Daughters of Abraham, and began working as an intern with the Multi-Cultural Alliance, where I developed programs for interfaith dialogue. Through each connection made, each story I heard, and each interaction I observed, I learned more about different religious traditions, as well as how to build relationships grounded in humility and curiosity.

Perhaps these are the skills that inspired me to embark on learning about racism and religious difference at the museum that January day, and to respond to a critical email with openness to the possibility of learning and growth. Over the more than twenty years since my first adventure beyond my familiar world, I have found my greatest joy and learning in embracing a sense of curiosity. The patient, grace-filled process and practice of curiously stepping into new spaces with a sense of wonder, possibility, and humility has now become my primary posture in faith, politics, and connecting across divisions.

"I have no special talents, I am only passionately curious."
—attributed to Albert Einstein

"The important thing is not to stop questioning…Never lose a holy curiosity."—attributed to Albert Einstein

"Ever since Darwin, we have had to come to terms with the fact that we share with our primate cousins the same three basic drives: [for] food, sex, and shelter. But humans possess…a fourth drive. Pure curiosity is unique to human beings. When animals sniff around in bushes, it's because they're looking for the three other things. It's only people, as far as we know, who look up at the stars and wonder what they are.[7]

"Our oldest stories about curiosity are warnings: Adam and Eve and the apple of knowledge, Icarus and the Sun, Pandora's Box. Early Christian theologians railed against curiosity: Saint Augustine claimed that 'God fashioned hell for the inquisitive.' Even humanist philosopher Erasmus suggested that curiosity was greed by a different name. For most of Western history, it has been regarded as a distraction at best, and at worst a poison that is corrosive to the soul and to society…A society that values order above all else will suppress curiosity. But a society that believes in progress,

---

[7] John Lloyd, quoted in Ian Leslie, *Curious: The Desire to Know and Why Your Future Depends on It* (New York: Basic Books, 2014), http://motivatedmastery.com/how-to-cultivate-curiosity/.

innovation, and creativity will cultivate it, recognizing that the inquiring minds of its people constitute its most valuable asset."[8] —John Lloyd, pitching a show called QI to the BBC

Questions for Reflection

1. Recall a time when you followed your curiosity. What was the result?

2. What obstacles do you experience in following the path of curiosity?

3. What circumstances do you require to provide space for curiosity?

[8]Ian Leslie, *Curious: The Desire to Know and Why Your Future Depends on It* (New York: Basic Books, 2014), http://motivatedmastery.com/how-to-cultivate-curiosity/

6

Showing Up:
Friendship as a Political Act

On the morning of Sunday, June 12, 2016, the first thing I did on waking up was to check my phone, a habit I would love to break. The night before, fifty people had been shot at a nightclub in Orlando. My thoughts immediately went to *Not again,* and then, *I hope the shooter wasn't Muslim.* I feared any perceived confirmation of anti-Muslim bias. I went downstairs and turned on the news to see now-all-too-familiar horrific images of a mass shooting: close-ups of young people in shock, tears running down their faces, recollecting each horrible moment from the first shots to the chaotic escapes, the moments of wondering whether their friends and loved ones had escaped and of hearing cell phones ringing from the floor of the club.

As more details began to emerge, I learned that the shooter was indeed a Muslim man. Although he was clearly afflicted and his motives far more complicated than religious extremism, the horrific violence was automatically declared an act of terrorism, simply because he was Muslim. Further, the victims were in a gay Latinx dance club, space typically regarded as a haven of safety and acceptance for those in the LGBTQ community

My stomach sank. I immediately knew this would feel deeply personal for each of my LGBTQ, Muslim, and Latinx friends and fellow partners in advocacy and equality work. I sent a message to my friends from the Colorado Muslim Society to assure them I was thinking of them. I am familiar with the backlash they receive after every such incident. I sent a message to my friend, the director of our largest LGBTQ advocacy organization, to let him know that I was grieving with him, cared for him, and was holding his community in my heart, a community that would surely be feeling the pain of this act of violence in a particular way.

Meanwhile, I had kids to wake up for a 10:00 a.m. soccer game. Although the world stops for those who are experiencing the immediacy of an act of violence, for most others life keeps going. It can feel dizzying to move between my various worlds: being emotionally present to those who are suffering, watching the horrific events unfold, and maintaining a sense of normalcy for the children I am parenting. Deciding how much to share with them and how much to hold back can be confusing and overwhelming. I feel the need to ensure that my kids have a sense of the imperative to work for justice and peace in their lives and their communities, but I also do not want to expose them to trauma they cannot yet process. So most often I watch news reports discreetly on my phone, move into the next room to console a friend who is grieving, and slip away to do what has become an unexpected but regular aspect of my work: leading community vigils in times of public tragedy.

This Sunday morning, just after driving to the soccer field, my phone rang, and the planning began. The first call was from Qusair, from the Colorado Muslim Society. All of the imams from across the state of Colorado would be gathering for a press conference to denounce this horrific act of violence. Qusair wanted to ensure that the LGBTQ community knew that Muslims were standing in deep solidarity with them, and he knew I had the relationships to connect the two groups. The next call was from Dave, the head of the LGBTQ advocacy organization. He was starting to plan a vigil and wanted to ensure that the Muslim community was being invited to speak and attend and that this act of violence by one sick person did not divide two communities that both experience marginalization. I sent text messages to connect the two groups and called our contacts in the media to give them a heads-up that the two events would be happening.

We gathered at one o'clock that afternoon at the Colorado Muslim Society, the room packed with people from the Muslim community, leaders from the LGBTQ community, interfaith leaders, people standing in solidarity with all of us, and news cameras. The imams seated at a long table in the front of a crowded room once again clarified that Islam does not condone let alone sanctify acts of terror (a clarification they have had to provide far too many times—whereas no Christian or white person is required to do the same after a shooting perpetrated by a white Christian male). People from the LGBTQ community reiterated that acts of violence would not divide us, and that in our community we would not perpetuate hatefulness.

Later that evening, we gathered with thousands of people who came to grieve at our local nightclub that was known as a safe haven for people in our LGBTQ community. We sang songs, held lighted candles, and I spoke alongside a rabbi and an imam as well as a dozen community leaders. I had the opportunity to talk, as a Christian pastor, to people from the LGBTQ community who have too often heard only words of judgment and condemnation from Christian leaders. From the stage in a gay nightclub I shared words expressing our heartbreak at lives lost early that morning in Florida, as well as sorrow for the ideology that has perpetuated pain and violence toward those who are LGBTQ. I named the light that each of us hold in our hands and in our hearts, and spoke of the deep humanity we share.

We were able to show up for one another that day because we had been showing up for one another for years. Over the previous two years, I had been working at the state Capitol alongside my friends from our state LGBTQ advocacy organization to ensure persons' rights were not diminished and that "religious freedom" was not used to justify discrimination against and dehumanization of people. I had been working for years with friends in our Muslim community to build relationships across our religious differences and to educate the community about anti-Muslim bias. In our shared work, we had become friends. We had shared meals and stories. We had visited one another's faith communities; we knew one another's hometowns and family stories. We had real friendships rooted in our stories and were committed to creating a stronger community together. So when the news alert came, along with the time to stand together in solidarity, showing up for one another was an assumption and a well-honed practice.

* * * *

Through years of advocacy and being a pastor in the community, I have learned that the single most important act is *showing up*. Navigating fear, embracing curiosity, and showing up for one another provide a foundation for transformation. Showing up requires first putting ourselves in proximity of another, then seeing "the other," building friendship, and acting in solidarity.

There is nothing more important than the effort to build real friendships and place our body in the proximity of other people. The effort of getting together with another person is transformative, far beyond what posting on social media or observing from behind a screen can be. Looking into someone's eyes, holding them in a compassionate hug, or sitting across a table for a shared coffee or meal builds trust and deepens connections in ways that nothing else does. Showing up and forming real friendships takes time and intentionality. Showing up and developing mutual friendships can also be seen as countercultural political acts, ones that are central to a thriving democracy in a time when we quickly retreat to our corners and isolate ourselves in our comfortable homes behind mind-numbing screens.

The Religious Call to Show Up

Behind every religion's command to *love your neighbor as yourself* are stories that ask, Who is my neighbor? And what does love look like? In one of the more provocative stories in the Hebrew Bible, the story of Ruth exemplifies how a deep relationship across difference can be mutual, faithful, and political. Ruth is a Moabite woman who, after her husband dies, follows her Israelite mother-in-law, Naomi, into the community of Jewish people with the vow: "Where you go, I will go; Where you lodge, I will lodge; your people shall be my people, and your God my God" (Ruth 1:16). Although Ruth could have returned to her Moabite people, she felt a commitment to stay with Naomi and navigate the uncertain road ahead together with her.

Ruth and Naomi are clever and faithful women who are in a culture where a woman's survival depends on a male son or husband. When the two women find themselves without a clear path to either, they navigate complicated systems of inheritance, land ownership, and coverture to find a way to stay together and to do what is necessary to survive. While still strategizing the path to their survival, the women assert the rights of the poor to glean the leftovers of the barley harvest and create a way to Naomi's family land. The friendship, commitment, and cleverness of Ruth and Naomi result in Ruth's pregnancy with Obed, who will be the father of Jesse, who will be the father of King David. The story of Ruth is a compelling story in the Jewish tradition and is read each year in the celebration of Shavuot. Ruth's story, rooted in deep friendship, calls people to faithfulness, loyalty, and ethical justice-seeking action.

In Christianity, the life of Jesus is primarily a story of "showing up." God shows up in the world as a baby to a young, unmarried, outsider mother. God shows up in the messiness of humanity and challenges assumptions and reminds people what the law of the Torah looks like in embodied form to challenge unjust systems. In the life and teaching of Jesus, we see that physical presence is core to finding healing and mutual liberation. Again and again, the face-to-face encounter between Jesus and those seeking relief from illness, hunger, poverty, or death brings healing and transforms lives. The parable of the Good Samaritan, of course, directly addresses the ways in which showing up and taking action are core to the practice of Christianity. A lawyer asks Jesus what he must do to inherit eternal life. Jesus responds with a question: "What is written in the law?" The man answers: "You shall love the Lord your God with all your heart, and with all your soul, and with all your strength, and with all your mind; and your neighbor as yourself." Jesus responds, "You have given the right answer; do this, and you will live" (Luke 10:25–28, paraphrased).

Understandably, the lawyer wants to know more. So he asks, "And who is my neighbor?" Jesus responds with the now familiar story: "A man was going down from Jerusalem to Jericho, and fell into the hands of robbers, who stripped him, beat him, and went away, leaving him half dead." Jesus goes on to name the multiple people—a priest and a Levite, people who should be upstanding ethical figures—who not only pass by the man in need but deliberately cross to the other side of the road to avoid the man further. Eventually, a Samaritan—an outcast in the Jewish community—walks by and is moved with pity. Not only does he go directly to the man in need, he also cleans and bandages his wounds, disinfects and treats them with oil and wine, loads the man onto his own animal, and takes him to safety in a nearby inn. He uses his own resources to ensure that the innkeeper will continue to provide a safe place for the man to heal (Luke 10:29–35, paraphrased).

The good Samaritan was the one who showed up and took action in a time of need, regardless of the circumstances. He broke social convention and let go of any fear for his own risk in helping the man who has been beaten. In telling the story, Jesus himself engaged in a political act. Political norms of the time were reliant on who was clean, pure, and worthy. Jesus raises the moral and ethical bar, calling us to move beyond rules and instead to center the health and well-being of the community. He challenges authority and the presumed piety of religious leaders to call people to a higher law.

For Albanian Muslims, Besa is a code of honor deeply rooted in faith and culture that demands a person take responsibility for the lives of others in difficult times. In some ways, it parallels the biblical commandment "Love your neighbor as yourself." For Muslims, this also echoes a core text from the Qur'an: "O mankind! We created you from a single pair of a male and a female and made you into nations and tribes, that you may know each other (not that you may despise each other). Verily the most honored of you in the sight of God is the most righteous of you. And God has full knowledge and is well acquainted (with all things)" (49:13, Yousef Ali). During World War II, the deeply engrained valuing of one another and the teaching of Besa saved lives as Muslim families risked their own lives to hide their Jewish friends from Nazi persecution. Albanians saved more than two thousand Jews from the Nazis, giving them clothes, names to disguise their identities, and incorporation into their own families. Across religious traditions, we find teachings that call us to see and honor the deep humanity of our neighbors, regardless of any differences.

What Does Showing Up Look Like?

Building relationships across differences takes intentional effort and can be personally challenging. The radical act of showing up often begins as an awkward encounter as we make ourselves vulnerable to another person. Every new contact involves a risk of rejection, embarrassment, looking ignorant, or saying the wrong thing. And every act of showing up holds the possibility of an unknown future. Building trust requires showing up again and again, and following through on commitments to move toward mutual transformation.

During my time in seminary, I built friendships with people from multiple religious traditions. The first time I was invited to attend a meeting at the local mosque in Fort Worth, I drove up to the large building, parked in a lot that didn't feel very different from the ones next to churches that I was used to, and walked up to the large glass doors. When I walked in, I was invited to remove my shoes and place them in a small cubby, and was handed a scarf to cover my head. I exhaled my slight nervousness and fear of embarrassing myself, covered my head, and walked into the open area of the mosque to gather at a table with women who were Jewish and Muslim, Baptist and Catholic. I quickly met a young woman in a hajib, Alia, who was funny and welcoming and invited me to take a seat next to her. At the end of the gathering I was invited to join the group the following week for kabob, grilled vegetables, rice, and baklava in the home of a Pakistani woman in the group. Over the next few years I would build friendships with women from many backgrounds. These relationships would shape me in ways that would become foundational in my personal and vocational life.

When I moved back home to Colorado to embark on work as a pastor, I grieved the relationships I was losing. I wondered how I would ever build the kind of relationships I had experienced without the seed of my seminary network.

Among the first calls I made upon starting my new ministry was to the local Council of Churches. I let the director know of my experiences and asked how I might get involved with interfaith leaders in Denver. He was happy to connect me to the religious advisory council for the University of Denver and invited me to join a local rabbi and clergy study group.

In those early days in my new hometown, I attended every event I could find at which I might meet people who were eager to build relationships across our religious differences. I participated at the local Turkish Muslim group's interfaith gatherings, visited a local synagogue, and asked other younger clergy from different religious backgrounds if we might meet for lunch. Sure, I often felt awkward or unsure about entering new spaces where others had known one another for years. Sure, I observed cultural differences between "interfaith" work in Fort Worth, Texas, where I had been in seminary, and in Denver, Colorado. Sure, I had some awkward interactions and made assumptions about people that were later proven false. Yet with each gathering, meeting, or event I attended, I met new people and formed new connections. By showing up, listening with humility, and engaging with a sense of openness, I was taking the first steps to building real relationships of solidarity and resilience.

A couple of years later when I began my work with the Interfaith Alliance of Colorado, I was immediately able to call upon the relationships I had already formed with leaders from multiple faith traditions. Those same skills and *ways of being* that had been nurtured by building relationships across religious differences helped me connect with people in human rights and political advocacy circles as well. In reflecting on the key skills and *ways of being* that support connecting across differences, I see that it is vital that we *see* one another clearly, build *friendships* that are authentic, and *act* in solidarity.

Seeing

Generally when I walk into a room, I first look around and size up the situation. After looking for people I know, I make quick judgements consciously and subconsciously. I decide who I want to talk to and who I want to avoid. However, I have started to interrupt this process and ask myself a few questions" Why am I drawn to this person and not that one? What assumptions am I making about others? Am I more inclined to place myself next to people who look like me or who look different than me? Why? The answers to these questions reveal my own implicit bias. Implicit bias is the attitudes or stereotypes that affect our understanding and actions in an unconscious way. The way we see others has been shaped by the stories that have been handed to us, whether we know it or not.

Implicit bias is personal, as I feel it in my own life and relationships; and it is systemic, because these little decisions we each make on our own build up in our community policies and our laws. Implicit bias affects the way we cross the street at the sight of someone deemed dangerous, the decisions we make when hiring someone, the classroom in which a child is placed, or the frequency with which someone is pulled over by the police and treated with violence. The way we see people has implications and has been woven into our systems in which people with deep unchallenged implicit bias are often in positions of power.

If we are to experience mutual liberation, we must change the way we see. I have found that this is only possible when I slow down and reflect. When I am moving quickly and unconsciously, I fall into old patterns and become incognizant of the ways my bias is keeping me from moving out of my comfort zone and into friendship with people who are different from me. When it comes down to it, there is mystery, possibility, and risk involved in *any* relationship. This is true in family relationships, in parenting, in being a neighbor, in meeting people who are very different from us, and in engaging people in the community in advocacy work. Human interaction always involves being vulnerable and opening ourselves to both potential joy and potential harm. When we slow down and interrupt our assumptions about people, we may be surprised.

Friendship

Ideally, when we take time truly to *see* another person, we recognize their inherent dignity and worth. When we learn each other's stories, pain, and hopes, we can build friendships strong enough to assure mutual well-being. Writing in *The Politics of Friendship*, philosopher Jacques Derrida peeled back the layers of identity, difference, and politics to remind us of one of the most fundamental truths and transformative acts: Friendship—mutually seeing and holding responsibility for one another—has the power to transform lives and societies. Interestingly, Derrida was a Jew, born in Algeria in 1930. As a child, he experienced discrimination and anti-Semitism. This shaped his opportunities and his experience of life and formed the foundation of his thinking.[1]

---

[1] Jacque Derrida, *The Politics of Friendship*, trans. George Collins (London; New York: Verso, 1997).

Friendship, from Derrida's view, is an amicable, ethical, and political relationship that requires a 'turning toward' one another in a biomechanical act with the underlying intentional impulse to decide to face another. Inevitable in the physical turning is the fact that we also have our backs to one another, leaving parts of ourselves as unknowable and vulnerable to the other. This is a reality that must be experienced. Simultaneously, through a face-to-face relationship, we come to see one another in ways that can only be experienced physically. In seeing one another and listening to one another, we feel the deep humanity of one another. When I drove to Fleming, Colorado with Iman, Ismail, and Ismail, we were each transformed by the acts of sitting together in a circle, seeing one another's facial expressions, being in one another's presence, and hearing one another's stories.

Friendship transcends demands for assimilation, acculturation, or simply occupying the same space. It invites transformation through navigation and invention of new ways of being together where both people are changed in some way. I have been forever changed through friendships with people like Alia, Iman, Qusair, Dave, and Harold and Claudia. Each of these friendships has changed the way I see and hear. Through Harold and Claudia I learned that our histories are communal. I learned to challenge notions of individualistic experiences, knowing that we carry the history of our communities in our bodies. Through Dave and my LGBTQ friends I have learned about gender identity, and the experienced differences between sexuality and gender, and the importance of honoring a person's full complex identity. Through Alia and Iman I have learned resilience and clarity in the midst of adversity.

We each give and take through first listening and coming to know one another. We eventually find ourselves taking on some pieces of the other, and sharing some parts of ourselves. Through friendship, we find that we are profoundly connected and interdependent, regardless of our differences. Like the Albanian Muslims who risked their own lives to take in their Jewish neighbors, we recognize that this connection moves beyond family, or ethnicity, or country. It is a deeply human interconnectedness. This is a radical truth that has the power to challenge assumptions, break down walls, challenge notions of who is "in" or "out," citizen or noncitizen. This is the love and relationship to which we are called, and it is a personal and political act.

Derrida sees friendship as a foundation for a democracy of the future. Rather than refining a current understanding of democracy, he sees this kind of friendship transcending the ways in which democracy has been restricted by definitions of nation-state and citizenship. The promise of democracy is freedom, equality, freedom of speech, and freedom of the press. For Derrida, these are not mere promises of the future, but imperatives that we are obliged to act on immediately. At the center of the possibility of living in this vision of democracy is friendship.

Aristotle named friendship as one of life's most essential virtues. He suggested that it plays an organizing role in the definition of justice and democracy. Aristotle described friendship as a relationship between two people in which love and goodwill are shared and reciprocated. He named three sources of goodwill in friendship: utility, pleasure, and wishing good for the other. For Aristotle, the perfect friendship is one in which friends love each other for their own sake, and they want good things for the other. Friendship can begin as one of pleasure (we are friends because she makes me laugh), or for practical purposes (we are friends because he drives my kids to soccer practice). Although these friendships may seem shallow or easily dissolved, they can evolve into deeper friendships of shared goodwill. The highest form of friendship is one in which there is reciprocal care, concern, and action to assure the goodwill of the other. Such friendships are resilient and lasting and have the power to transform. Aristotle had a very high view of friendship, believing that its importance supersedes even justice and honor. He found friendship to be the glue that keeps cities and societies together.

When we see ourselves as deeply connected to one another as friends, we challenge the artificial lines that have been drawn to cause division. Instead, we recognize that we are connected. We find that we cannot sit idly by as families are separated and children are placed in cages at our southern U.S. border. We cannot watch silently as rights are stripped from transgender people or women. As we develop real friendships, we begin to feel the pain others feel as they are placed in detention centers or are singled out by police based on the color of their skin. When we care so deeply about the well-being of another that we can no longer stand silently by, friendship becomes political.

Acting

If seeing and entering into relationships is the foundation of friendships and moving into our more profound shared humanity, *acting* is how we build trust and create lasting change. Our faith traditions call us to act in ways that honor and support one another. In Matthew 7:24–27, Jesus differentiates between *hearers* and *doers*:

> "Everyone then who hears these words of mine and acts on them will be like a wise man who built his house on rock. 25 The rain fell, the floods came, and the winds blew and beat on that house, but it did not fall, because it had been founded on rock. And everyone who hears these words of mine and does not act on them will be like a foolish man who built his house on sand. The rain fell, and the floods came, and the winds blew and beat against that house, and it fell—and great was its fall!"

Judaism and Islam are both religions rooted in action. The instruction to recognize the Sabbath reminds Jews to set aside time to engage in physical acts to celebrate and remember God. They light candles, sing, eat bread and drink wine, and relish one another's presence. Shifting from frenzy to focused attention is an act of commitment. Rabbi Abraham Joshua Heschel famously said he was "praying with his feet" when marching with Dr. Martin Luther King, Jr., to stand up against the forces of racism, segregation, and hatred. Islam requires followers to stop what they are doing five times a day to practice the embodied act of bowing to God in prayer and to submit to peace through their daily thoughts and actions. The way we use our bodies to pray, to march, to vote, to show up for one another with compassion speaks to our deepest values.

As we know far too well, school shootings in the U.S. usually elicit from politicians and community leaders the tired refrain that their thoughts and prayers are with the victims. We want more. So we vote and we urge others to vote for leaders who will *act*. We demand leaders who will study the problem, create real gun safety laws, invest in the social-emotional well-being of our kids, and fund safety nets that make our communities stronger. This real gun violence emergency requires *real* action.

In one of the most profound writings of Martin Luther King, Jr.— his "Letter from Birmingham Jail"—King expresses his exhaustion with the "white moderate church," which was not only refusing to act but also critiquing King's actions as extreme and untimely. In his letter, King wrote:

> All that is said here grows out of a tragic misconception of time. It is the strangely irrational notion that there is something in the very flow of time that will inevitably cure all ills. Actually time is neutral. It can be used either distructively [sic] or constructively. I am coming to feel that the people of ill-will have used time much more effectively than the people of goodwill. We will have to repent in this generation not merely for the vitriolic words and actions of the bad people, but for the appalling silence of the good people. We must come to see that human progress never rolls in on wheels of inevitability. It comes through the tireless efforts of men willing to be co-workers with God, and without this hard work time itself becomes an ally of the forces of social stagnation. We must use time creatively and forever realize that the time is always ripe to do right. Now is the time to make real the promise of democracy, and transform our pending national elegy into a creative psalm of brotherhood. Now is the time to lift our national policy from the quicksand of racial injustice to the solid rock of human dignity.[2]

A thriving democracy requires active participation to become an actual "more perfect union." Participation entails a continual process of learning, listening, reflecting, acting, and learning, listening, and acting again. Non-action is the enemy of democracy and the antithesis of what it means to live into the core values of our faith traditions, which call us to love one another. In *The*

---

[2]Martin Luther King Jr., "Letter from the Birmingham Jail," written on April 16, 1963, to seven other clergymen. Quote is from original typewritten letter, online at http://okra.stanford.edu/transcription/document_images/undecided/630416-019.pdf . Reprinted in many books with slight alterations to the text.

Banality of Evil,[3] political philosopher Hannah Arendt explores how the inaction of seemingly "good people" led to the evil of the Holocaust. A young Jewish woman in Nazi Germany, Arendt saw firsthand how people she had regarded as friends failed to think, stand up, and speak out in the face of a murderous fascist regime. From religious leaders, professors, and politicians to prison guards and workers in concentration camps, people followed morally corrupt orders rather than acting on their core values. Beyond evil intent was a simple failure to think and act for moral good.

Reclaiming the Power of Showing Up

Showing up for one another is a way of reclaiming power. Showing up for one another is living into a more accurate story than the stories of division and self-reliance that we have been taught. By recognizing our interconnected common humanity, developing real friendships in unexpected places, and acting out of deep solidarity, we move toward greater thriving together.

Questions for Reflection

1. What does it mean to you when someone shows up for you?

2. What prevents you from showing up?

3. When have you developed an unexpected friendship? What was its impact on your life? On your friend's life?

4. When have you come to see a person in a new way?

5. When have you shown up to a challenging space? What happened?

---

[3]Hannah Arendt, *Eichmann in Jerusalem: A Report on the Banality of Evil* (New York: Viking Press, 1963).

7

Broken: Messing Up

In the days immediately following the presidential inauguration of Donald Trump, people in my circles wanted to act, and they wanted to move *now*. Trump released new executive orders in quick succession, each new decree worse than the last. On Friday, January 27, one week after taking office, he gave an executive order that suspended resettlement of Syrian refugees, paused overall refugee resettlement, and barred non-citizens from seven Muslim majority countries from traveling to the U.S. This was the "Muslim ban" that Trump had threatened and that so many had feared. Protestors quickly started organizing online to meet at the airport to protest the ban and ensure that those who were already in the air—many of whom had been waiting for years for entry to the U.S. as a refugee—would indeed be allowed to enter.

Meanwhile, I was on my way to spend the night at Fort Collins with my family (all of whom supported Trump) to celebrate my sister's birthday. I felt the tension in my bones: I longed to be at the airport with my friends and partners in the advocacy issues about which I care deeply, and I was also grateful to be with my sister and our family, whom I genuinely love. After singing "Happy Birthday" and sharing cake, I snuck to the basement to watch live videos of what was happening at the airport and sent messages of solidarity to let friends know I was with them in spirit. The ACLU led the charge to ensure that people were not held at the airport and to challenge the legality of the ban that would be fought in the courts. Meanwhile, the rest of us struggled with what to do next.

In the days that followed, messages swirled regarding what we could possibly do to express our anger at the executive order and our solidarity with the Muslim and refugee communities. Everyone wanted to do something, but no one was sure who would lead. There were clear calls locally and across the country to create space for younger and newer leaders to bring their creativity and vision. My phone rang with people wanting to be a part of whatever wound up being organized. By Wednesday it looked as if a group of young leaders had stepped up to lead a rally to "Stand with our Muslim neighbors," and our organization, the Interfaith Alliance of Colorado, followed. The rally was scheduled for four days later, on a Saturday morning. The group asked me to put together a group of interfaith leaders to speak at the rally. Simultaneously, the rabbi of our largest synagogue reached out and asked if he could play music and be a part of the rally to express his heartbreak and solidarity. He said that although the rally had been planned for the exact same time as Saturday morning Shabbat services, he was inviting the entire congregation to attend the rally and stand in support of the Muslim and refugee communities. It was a big deal.

On Thursday and Friday of that week, I sent out requests trying to identify faith leaders who would be a good fit to bring a message of solidarity and resilience at this time. At short notice, I was able to invite a Sikh woman who was a leader in her community, the rabbi who had asked to participate, and a Christian pastor who was passionate about refugee support. As an organization, we helped spread the word about the event and invited all of our partners to attend. That Saturday morning, as I was preparing to head to Civic Center Park for the rally, I received a text that my sister-in-law had gone into labor. My brother-in-law asked if I would help by picking up his wife's mother from the airport that afternoon and then taking her to the hospital. Of course, I said yes. I love them dearly and was excited to meet another nephew. I then got in the car to head to the rally, hoping to be able to "do it all."

When I arrived at Civic Center Park, made my way through thousands of people, and wound around to the back of the stage, I saw that the rally was chaotic and disorganized, as were many gatherings at the time. There wasn't a clear agenda, and far more people expected to speak than there was time for speeches with any real depth and vision. There were too many politicians and not enough people who had experienced life marginalized as a Muslim person or a refugee. The vast majority of people from the Muslim community who participated were Arabic Muslims and not Black or African Muslims. Further, after a slew of political leaders shared their thoughts, the mayor spoke to give his support to Muslim and refugee communities. This same mayor was under intense scrutiny by our organization and our advocacy partners for his "camping ban" that criminalized people for being homeless by moving and ticketing people out of public spaces. Then it was my turn. I led my part of the rally, side by side with a rabbi, a Sikh leader, and a Christian pastor, then hustled to my car, to the airport, and then to the hospital to meet my new baby nephew.

As I walked into the hospital, I made the mistake of looking down at my phone. I had received multiple emails from people who were expressing their frustration with several details of the rally, a rally some thought I had planned. One email in particular set me fuming. A man I considered a friend was furious that the rabbi who had spoken was from a synagogue that has supporters from AIPAC, a conservative Jewish pro-Israel lobby (it is a large, diverse synagogue with people from both ends of the political spectrum). As a liberal Jew critical of the role of Israel in Palestine, he was incensed that I would have allowed this rabbi to speak. I was shocked by his response, as I had both known and respected the rabbi for years and seen him in a relationship with my Palestinian friends. Further, I thought it was short-sighted to critique the largest synagogue in town, whose congregants chose to miss Shabbat service to show solidarity with the Muslim community. This friend also said some hurtful things implying that we as an organization were putting on a show rather than engaging in relationships, an attack that couldn't have been further from the truth given our daily work.

The subsequent emails and social media messages were critical of the fact that the mayor had expressed support for refugees while criminalizing Denverites who were experiencing homelessness at that very moment. This was a valid critique, and it highlighted more significant strategic and relational questions that needed to be asked. Finally, some of my friends from the black community were angry that black Muslim and refugee voices had been marginalized at the rally. I read the messages and noticed the ways in which the words quickly went into my body and set my head spinning. I took a breath or three and decided I would return to the messages *after* meeting my new nephew.

I went up the elevator to the third floor, first hugged my three-year-old nephew, congratulated him on becoming a big brother, and then wrapped my arms around the sweet newborn boy who was my new nephew. Welcome to the world, sweet baby! It's a complicated, chaotic mess. And it will be ok, *we will all be ok*. And I love you.

* * * *

On Monday morning I arrived at work to find a team of staff who were confused, fuming, and frustrated. Some did not understand why there was such a strong critique of the rally. Others felt that the rally had portrayed underlying ignorance and racism in the planning and implementation. With tensions running high, I set aside everything we had planned for the day and dedicated our time to trying to understand what the underlying issues had been. We waded into the complexity of supporting new organizers (the group of young leaders), who may not have had either strong relationships in the community or an understanding of the underlying personal and political dynamics at play.

Additionally, when we—mostly Christian, Jewish, or agnostic folks—are working to confront Islamophobia and stand in solidarity with our Muslim neighbors, we are often ignorant of the internal tensions and power differences within Muslim communities. In Denver particularly, there are undoubtedly cultural and language differences, as well as a high number of African immigrants and people for whom English is not their first language. Some people have been here for a generation or more, others for only a few months or years. Some in the immigrant and refugee communities have positive relationships with law enforcement and politicians, as they rely on these systems to provide safety. However, many of my friends in the black community have experienced police as untrustworthy and dangerous. In the dominant culture we tend to make sweeping generalizations or tokenize people while claiming to be "supporting" them.

As a staff, we processed the multiple layers of pain, brokenness, and anger that many people being targeted were feeling now, and the pain, brokenness, and anger of those who have spent generations being dehumanized by inadequate and unjust policies, toxic white supremacy, and the culture of Christian supremacy. We discussed the complexity of navigating these realities at the same time as trying to bring about systemic change. We named the sense of urgency we felt about confronting dehumanizing policies. We recognized that our sense of urgency often prevented us from ensuring that our methods matched our values and our hopes. We decided that we needed to apologize to those in the community who had been hurt and frustrated by the rally, and that we needed to come to internal clarity about how to navigate these spaces better. Through this work, we developed the following public statement:

Leading in This Time

We are in a wild time. A time when organizations such as the Interfaith Alliance of Colorado are navigating how to lead. We are learning how to stand in solidarity with those most marginalized and at risk, and seeking to move others toward "resistance."

A recurring aspiration for us has been that all of us reflect on the ways racism, sexism, homophobia and other deeply embedded "isms" and "phobias"—which are present within progressive movements—will be called forth, addressed, and eliminated.

We are learning.

As an organization we seek to always prioritize standing with the marginalized as we work together to support faith and freedom. We bring people together from multiple faith (and non-faith) backgrounds to work for human rights and equity. This is big, messy, and at times, overwhelming work.

We name that as we lead, there are times we have rushed to action before we have time to thoroughly assure we are fully living into our values. Specifically, we seek to ensure that people from marginalized communities (black, brown, immigrant, refugee, religious minorities, GLBTQ, ability, gender, economic poverty) are at the center of our relationships and our work. We seek to connect people in multiple congregations and communities to this work.

We hope to model how we can move at a pace that this critical moment in history requires, while also remaining faithful to our core values of solidarity with those marginalized, freedom, equality, civility, and respect for differences. Central to this work is humility and commitment to relationship with one another and with the community. There are times we choose to be strategic in order to achieve our goals, and there are times we let go of end goals to maintain integrity. We name that there are inherent tensions and sacrifices we make each day when choosing to work in or participate in particular spaces. We navigate these decisions in community, evaluate and adjust as needed, while prioritizing right-relationship.

In this light, we will ask the following questions before committing our name and our voice to public events:

- *What is the end goal of the event?*

- *Are people of color active participants in planning and speaking in this event?*

- *Are black people specifically active participants in this event?*

- *Will multiple experiences, stories and perspectives be represented (GLBT, religious diversity, racial diversity)?*

- *Are there action steps for follow up after the event? If so, what are they?*

- *Are power-holders/influencers involved? If so, will they be held accountable for their record? How?*

- *Is the primary organizer a "grass-roots" or a "grass-tops" organization?*

- *Are there grassroots organizations that share a similar mission? Have they been consulted?*

- *Have safety precautions been taken for the event? If so, what are they?*

We ask these questions because we believe it is important to be aligned with our values when deciding on our level of participation in events. We view each question with the inevitable tension and give-and-take which come with navigating how to make effective and sustainable change.[1]

---

[1]Interfaith Alliance Team, "Leading in This Time," (blog), Interfaith Alliance of Colorado website, February 15, 2017, https://interfaithallianceco.org/blog/2018/6/4/leading-in-this-time?rq=leading%20in%20this%20time.

* * * *

We are a part of a broken world. We live in a culture where people have been ranked one above another based on the color of their skin, the country of their birth, and their gender and sexuality. Additionally, we live in a culture that values output over process, profit over people, and what we have more than who we are. We can't help but be a part of these broken systems and the pieces of our culture that are toxic: It is the air we breathe. These realities set us up for further division and pain, and contribute to our mistakes and breaches of relationships. Sometimes our errors are obvious, such as when I say I will do something and I don't. Or when I write the wrong information in an email. Or when I do not prepare enough before giving a presentation. Sometimes our mistakes are hurtful to others, such as when I do not invite a person to a meeting or gathering and they feel left out. Or when I use words that are insensitive and hurtful to someone in the group.

Our mistakes can be personal, and they can be systemic and political. Often when engaging in the worlds of religion and politics, our mistakes are rooted in historical oppression and a deeply broken culture and broken relationships. If we are working for true mutual liberation, mistakes will be inevitable, for we are still learning to undo centuries of habits and painful assumptions that have been internalized and woven into our thought patterns and shared actions. In this context, it is easy to make mistakes and cause harm, less out of intention than out of ignorance. Regardless of intent, the *impact* is real, and our response must come from authenticity and a desire for repair.

In these contexts, where our personal actions have caused direct harm, it is vital that we recognize and accept our mistakes with humility, listening, and reflection. We must quickly take the necessary steps to correct the error and work to repair any harm or damage to relationships.

In one of the more humiliating experiences of my life, I said the wrong name in a prayer at a memorial service. It wasn't just any memorial service; it was a service at which public leaders, senators, national heads of organizations, and press were present in the wake of the shooting at Planned Parenthood in Colorado Springs. With about a thousand people who were hurt and mourning in the room, I was asked to do a prayer for those who had been killed, including a police officer who was killed protecting the community. As I believe it is vital that we say the names of those who have died, I was naming the people who had been killed. Except instead of saying "Officer Garret Swasey," I said, "Officer Patrick Swayze."

As the words left my lips, I realized what I had done, and my stomach sank, and my mind raced. I was clearly tired; it had been a long week, and my brain and heart were exhausted. I was feeling the pressure of the moment, and I made a mistake. A big mistake. In front of *a lot* of people. I was mortified and embarrassed. At the same time, I felt terrible that I had not actually said the name of the officer who had been killed. At that moment, as I was continuing the words of the prayer, in my mind I was trying to decide what to do next. Do I ignore it and act as if it didn't happen and hope people didn't notice? But I knew people had heard, and more than that, I knew I had not honored the man who had lost his life.

So at that moment, after I said, "Amen," I opened my eyes, looked out to the crowd, and named my mistake and apologized. I went on to share that I felt it was important to say the name of Officer Garrett Swazey, and appropriate or not, I tried to add levity by saying we also pray for Patrick Swayze, but that this was about the heroic action of Officer Garett Swazey. The crowd laughed and seemed put at ease, and I sat down, still feeling terrible for any harm I had caused, still mortified, and hoping the world wouldn't see this moment in a news clip or on *The Daily Show*.

After this experience, when I could breathe again, I reflected on what had caused that mistake. At root were exhaustion and inadequate preparation. I can learn from these mistakes and take steps to avoid making them in the future. I can be sufficiently self-aware to know when it is essential that I step away, slow down, and take time to center myself before speaking in public. I can take time in advance to read through my words and double-check all names and any words that might be more complex or confusing. When relationships have been breached, I can lean in rather than run away. I can set aside my ego and move beyond being "right" to being in right relationship. I can continually work to discern and center what is *actually* most important at this moment. Is it most important that I avoid personal embarrassment or that I say the name of the man who lost his life? Is it most important that I prove that I was right in sending the email, or inviting this person to speak, or is it most important that I heal the relationship and look toward partnerships in the future to achieve our shared hopes?

* * * *

We often avoid engaging in work and conversations around religion and politics because we are afraid of making mistakes. We are more scared of sounding ignorant, of disrupting or causing division, or of hurting someone we care about than about doing the right thing. Further, we see mistakes as hyper-personal and fail to acknowledge our participation in and perpetuation of systemic and historic brokenness that continue to cause harm. Both personal mistakes and involvement in systemic brokenness are inevitable. Silence and complicity can be as harmful as saying or doing the wrong thing. Rather than avoiding or running away for fear of making a mistake, we can see the work of righting our inevitable wrongs as an opportunity to practice building our skills at deepening relationships and living into the teachings of our multiple faiths, teachings that move us toward mutual liberation.

Mistakes (Sin) and Religious Wisdom

All religious traditions have something to say about mistakes or the inevitable harm we cause one another as humans. Many religious traditions use the term "sin" to speak of the break in relationship between people and God, and between people and one another. Further, in one way or another, almost all religious traditions speak about reconciliation, repair, forgiveness, and return to right relationship. Most religious traditions speak to both personal sin or breakdown in relationships as well as systemic or community sin or brokenness that perpetuates harm. Through sacred stories and shared instruction, we see that making mistakes and hurting one another and being caught up in cultural dysfunction are all human conditions with which we have been struggling since the beginning of humanity.

In Hinduism, an understanding of sin and forgiveness forms the basis of ethics and morality. Such an understanding's purpose is to facilitate the order and regularity of the world, enforcement of *dharma,* and the evolution of beings. Sin may arise from both intentional and unintentional actions and through negligence and ignorance. The three-fold impurities of egoism, attachments, and delusion are the leading causes of sin, which in turn lead to sinful behavior, suffering and ignorance, and delusion. The effects of actions build up in the body in ways that are either toxic or healing. Sin is seen as an impurity, which arises as an effect or consequence of one's evil actions and which can be neutralized through various yoga and transformative practices on the path of liberation (*moksha*). When we hurt ourselves, or other people (sins or *pāpams*), we are bound to the mortal world and subjected to repeated deaths and rebirths. Sinful actions result in painful realities in every area of our life and specifically of our health.

Reconciliation and forgiveness are also central in Hinduism and are referenced countless times throughout the Upanishads and the Vedas. Through facing the consequences of our actions, confessing, physical cleansing and fasting, performing rituals, praying and practicing mantras, visiting spiritual sites, bathing in sacred rivers, practicing yoga and meditation, seeking the wisdom of saints and gurus, and making charitable gifts, one can right the wrongs that have been caused and return to balance as poison is released from the body.

The Abrahamic faiths all have central teachings about the ways in which broken relationships with God and other people shape our lives and communities. In Judaism, the holiest day of the year, Yom Kippur, is devoted to communal repentance for sins committed over the previous year. Between Rosh Hashana and Yom Kippur, Jews are instructed to follow readings, prayers, and worship services that support efforts to make amends, wipe the slate clean, and begin again with loved ones, friends, and the broader community.

There are two categories of sin in Jewish thought: sins against God, and sins against other people. Sins against God can be ritual infractions, such as breaking the Sabbath, eating non-kosher food, or putting money over attention to God. Sins against other people can be personal acts, such as theft or gossip or adultery. One of the most profound breaches in Judaism is a failure to show hospitality to the stranger. Sins against God can be made right through prayer, charity, and fasting, but sins against people can only be made right through seeking amends with the one who has been harmed. The word for "returning to God" is *teshuvah* and involves confession, expression of regret, and vows not to repeat the misdeed. The global effort of teshuvah is connected to tikkun olam, or the call to "repair the world." This points to the systemic and communal work of repair that must be done to move into right relationship with God and one another for cosmic healing and liberation.

In Islam, mistakes and sin are seen as consequences of being human and are regarded as opportunities to grow closer to Allah. The Prophet Muhammad is known to have said, "All human beings make mistakes often. The best of those who make mistakes often are those who repent [to Allah]" (Hadith 2499, Tirmizi, paraphrased). Allah (God) is said to be most forgiving and merciful, and sin is not a cause for shame but an opportunity to correct flaws. Prophet Muhammad corrected people's missteps with gentleness, empathy, and creativity. He used mistakes as opportunities to empower people, not break them. A review of the life and teaching of the Prophet Muhammad in the Hadith exemplifies how Muslims are instructed to address the harm caused. Followers of Islam are taught to address mistakes directly and gently, to redirect people to focus on Allah, to avoid setting people up for failure, to use firmness when appropriate, and always to spare people's dignity.

Christianity reminds us that we are all born into a broken world. Although this knowledge can be distorted and used to promote further harm, I instead recognize it as naming our inevitable shortcomings and the damage that we cause one another, and as a call to work to bring justice and healing. Sin is a separation from God and from one another that can be experienced personally and systemically. What we experience as "mistakes" or sin are most often actions that diminish and demean people in one way or another. Jesus calls us to right relationship through seeing and acting for the full humanity and dignity of each and every person, especially those who have been marginalized, impoverished, and maligned. When we find that we have participated intentionally or unintentionally in degrading and dehumanizing others, we must take actions to repent, seek forgiveness, and repair the harm. For me, the words of Mary's Magnificat in the Gospel of Luke exemplify this call to right the mistakes and pain of the world.

Mary's Song of Praise

And Mary said,

"My soul magnifies the Lord,

and my spirit rejoices in God my Savior,

for he has looked with favor on the lowliness of his servant.
Surely, from now on all generations will call me blessed;

for the Mighty One has done great things for me,
and holy is his name.

His mercy is for those who fear him

from generation to generation.

He has shown strength with his arm;
he has scattered the proud in the thoughts of their hearts.

He has brought down the powerful from their thrones,
and lifted up the lowly;

he has filled the hungry with good things,
and sent the rich away empty.

He has helped his servant Israel,
in remembrance of his mercy,

according to the promise he made to our ancestors,
to Abraham and to his descendants forever."

—Luke 1:46–55

Brokenness in Politics

Of all our institutions, political institutions may be one of the least forgiving and most allergic to apologies. Although religious institutions have clearly caused great harm, at least they have built-in channels to address healing and repair (even if this is not always done well). In political life, healing, restoration, compassion, and love are too often shunned or seen as signs of weakness. How many leaders will take time to reflect, articulate their honest regret, and make efforts to repair the ways in which policies they wrote or supported caused harm? For example, how many leaders have apologized for how their aim to be tough on crime has in fact led to mass incarceration and the obliteration of families in black communities?

The painful reality is that our political system punishes self-awareness and rewards overconfidence, ego, and perceived "strength." Political professionals focus ahead and move at a pace that does not allow time for reflection, repair, or profound transformation. Unfortunately, political leaders who offer genuine public apologies or make an effort to right a wrong are declared "guilty," and political leaders who deny or ignore wrongdoing are merely in a short-term "controversy," their failings soon forgotten as we all keep moving forward.

In my work in political advocacy, I frequently run into conflicts in coalitions that are trying to bring about systemic change and dismantle institutionalized racism. This is an arduous task as the system itself was built in, for, and by a culture of racist ideology. We must play the game to change the laws (and improve people's lives), but the *act* of working within the broken system perpetuates and supports the system itself. This is a heartbreaking and frustrating truth of any work for social change that is rooted in values that honor human dignity and strive for equity and healing. When faced with this reality, we can either assimilate to the system, escape the system and choose not to participate at all (leaving others to experience the consequences), or commit to the long-haul work of seeking transformation within the system without succumbing to the broken system.

Creating Connection and Healing

This work of naming accountability and repairing and working for healing in the face of our own shortcomings and failures amid centuries of systemic oppression requires a commitment to building relationships across our differences in the face of our imperfections. To be able to do this hard work of repair, we must have a primary orientation toward a right relationship and care for the well-being of others, and specifically of those beyond our family, tribe, or in-group. Because such work is not automatic for us, it must be built and cultivated deliberately over time.

The best way that I have found to work through conflicts, mistakes, and harm I have caused is to engage in the real work of loving and building trusting relationships. This is not easy when the ego is involved. It is time-consuming and inconvenient. And it is easy to push challenging relationships off our priority list. Loving beyond ourselves means intentionally noticing thoughts that are harmful or dehumanizing to others and intervening in our own mental patterns so that we can once again recognize the full humanity of those with whom we are angry or frustrated. Creating connection means making time and going out of our way to put the needs of another first.

Our faith traditions teach that in the midst of personal breach of trust, mistake, or broken relationship, there are some key actions you can and must take to move back into a right relationship with God and others:

1. *Acknowledge the harm and the experience of those who have been harmed and what you did to cause them damage.* Without qualifications, admit you messed up. Take seriously what the injured tell you about *how they feel.* Any excuses you make for your action, as real as they may be, will not contribute to healing.

2. *Apologize clearly.* Do not say, "I'm sorry *if* you were hurt." That is not an actual apology.

3. *Identify steps you will take to avoid repeating this kind of mistake and ask those who are harmed what you must do to make things right.* Take time to reflect and to name the ways in which you will be more aware of the consequences of your actions in

future. Ask those who have been harmed what you can do to rebuild their trust.

4. *Don't demand forgiveness.* Trust takes longer to build than to break down. Healing hurt can take a while. Trust that forgiveness will come, and open yourself to receiving it if and when it is given.

5. *If you get off to a bad start, admit it, and stop digging.* Too often, people give excuses when they should instead acknowledge their responsibility. If you feel yourself doing this, stop, name what has happened, and start back at step one.

6. *Remember that in addressing a mistake, your goal is not to prove that you're right.* Even if you felt what you did wasn't wrong, clearly admit that it wasn't effective and even that it was hurtful. Peel back to understand the real goal. Quite often the goal is to be in right relationship, not to be *right.*

Healing in Politics

Without a doubt we are in a divisive time in our American history. At the root of much of our trauma and brokenness in the U.S. is institutionalized racism, cultural supremacy of whiteness, and the abuse of power and resources. This toxic culture is powerful precisely because it is always present and simultaneously difficult to name or identify. Even the simple act of naming this may feel painful and "divisive." As we navigate the divisions in our political system and work for collective liberation, it is important that we build countercultural practices in our home, family, and work life. The following characteristics are based on the work of Daniel Buford, a lead trainer with the People's Institute for Survival and Beyond, who has done extensive research on racism and white supremacy culture. These characteristics show up in the attitudes and behaviors of all of us—because they shape the very air we breathe. If we are to break through centuries of pain in order to experience real connection, freedom, and thriving, we must recognize and then transform the ways in which we have internalized and institutionalized these habits. In the left column are habits that are a part of a toxic culture, and on the right are antidotes that can help lead to healing.

Perfectionism	Antidote
Little appreciation for the work that others are doing, while focusing on inadequacies and mistakes. We have a tendency to see mistakes as tied to identity rather than as being a source for future learning.	We can develop a culture of appreciation, take time to make sure that people's work and efforts are appreciated, and separate the person from the mistake. Never compare our best to another person's worst.
Constant urgency	**Antidote**
Moving so fast that it is difficult to take time to be inclusive, encourage thoughtful decision-making, think long-term, and consider consequences.	Set realistic time expectations. Learn from past experience and be clear about how you will make the right decisions when in a hurry in a way that will allow space to think about the impact of actions on other people.
Only one right way	**Antidote**
The belief that there is one right way to do things, and that once people are pointed in the right direction, they will see the light and adopt that "one right way."	Work on developing the ability to notice when people do things differently and how those different ways might help you grow. Never assume that you know what's best for a community in isolation from meaningful relationships with that community.
Paternalism	**Antidote**
Those with power think they are capable of making decisions for and in the interests of those without power. Those without power understand they do not have it and understand who does.	Make sure everyone knows their level of responsibility and authority and include people who are affected by decisions in the decision-making process.

Either/or thinking	Antidote
Things are either/or: that is, good/bad, right/wrong, with us/against us. This results in trying to simplify complicated situations; for example, believing that poverty is simply a result of a lack of education.	Notice when people are simplifying complex issues, particularly when the stakes seem high. Slow down and encourage a more in-depth analysis.
Fear of open conflict	**Antidote**
Emphasis on being polite and equating the raising of troublesome issues with being impolite, rude, or out of line. When someone raises an issue that causes discomfort, the response is to blame the person for raising the issue rather than to look at what is actually causing the problem.	Distinguish between being polite and raising hard issues. Don't require those who raise hard questions to raise them in "acceptable" ways. Once a conflict is resolved, take the opportunity to revisit it and see how it might have been handled differently.
Individualism	**Antidote**
The assumption that we must do things on our own and pull ourselves up by our bootstraps. Individual recognition is more highly valued than cooperation. This leads to isolation and creates a lack of accountability.	Include teamwork as an essential value. Ask for help when you need it and become comfortable receiving support. Get to know your neighbors and coworkers in deeper, more connected ways.
More	**Antidote**
Success is always bigger. Progress equals expansion, regardless of how well people are cared for. Success gives no value, not even negative value, to its cost; for example, more consumption without thinking of the impact on the environment or the increase in income inequality.	Encourage Seventh Generation thinking by asking how the actions will affect people seven generations from now. Make sure that any cost/benefit analysis includes all the costs, not just the financial ones.

Objectivity	Antidote
The belief that there is such a thing as being objective or neutral. The idea that emotions are inherently destructive and irrational, and should not play a role in decision making or group process, thus invalidating people who show passion.	Realize that everybody has a worldview and that everybody's worldview affects the way they understand things. Realize that this includes you, too. Push yourself to sit with discomfort when people are expressing themselves in ways that are not familiar to you.
Right to comfort	**Antidote**
The belief that those with power have a right to emotional and psychological comfort. Scapegoating those who cause discomfort. Equating individual acts of unfairness against white people with systemic racism, which daily targets people of color.	Understand that discomfort is at the root of all growth and learning. Welcome it as much as you can. Deepen your political analysis of racism and oppression as systemic. Don't take everything personally.

* * * *

As we work within the context of broken systems and broken relationships, it is a good idea continually to take time to reflect, learn, seek healing, and embrace a posture of love. Collective liberation means seeing the ways in which we cause harm and working to make it right each and every day.

One of the most formative relationships in my life is with a friend who has pushed me to see and act in ways that challenge the systemic racism in which we all swim. Early on, as I began to lead the Interfaith Alliance of Colorado, in order to understand better the intersections of racism and religion, I hired a black woman who was an experienced community leader to join our team. I knew from the start that the power dynamics would be a challenge. Previously, we had been peers in our work, and now I, a white woman, was serving as the executive director of an organization, and she, a black woman, was in a role titled "program director." During the volatile time after the 2016 election, my friend made a Facebook post on our organization page that was not aligned with the voice of the organization for which I was responsible. When I saw the post, I knew it would be offensive to our members, and I quickly deleted it and called her to let her know I was removing it and why.

This did not go over well. As I shared my concern and let her know about the action I felt I had needed to take, my friend and employee become quiet. My stomach turned. I hated being in this position. She was upset, and I felt defensive. I knew the complexity of the situation right away. First was the power dynamic with me as a white woman being the "supervisor" of a black woman who had already been a peer and friend. Next, we had no clear social media guidelines or instructions in place. I had not communicated my expectations on that to her. Also, I had felt a sense of urgency and had deleted the post *before* making a phone call to let her know I was doing so. She felt that I, a white woman, had silenced her voice, as a black woman. This stirred historical trauma for her. I wondered about the standards that had made the post feel inappropriate to me; the content was accurate, though it was communicated in an abrasive way, and it was not from what I thought of as a reputable source. I felt that my responsibility as executive director of the organization made me accountable for the history and membership of the organization, and I prioritized this responsibility over our relationship. I felt the entire situation was morally ambiguous, and I wasn't sure whether I was *right* or *wrong,* but I knew we had to address the underlying power dynamics and historical pain.

We both realized we had set ourselves up for a toxic power dynamic. We knew the historical realities of an interfaith organization founded mainly by white progressive Christians. We knew the spirit of my friend as a black power truth-teller and someone whose integrity is tied to living her truth authentically— something I wanted to support and not diminish. After taking a bit of space to breathe and do what we needed to reflect and heal, we both leaned into the arduous conversation that needed to be had. We set up a time for coffee, and we each shared our experience. I apologized and named that I did not want to be in a position of censoring her voice and truth. I shared the complexity I felt in my responsibility to the organization, even as I was working diligently to shift the culture. She shared the pain the experience had stirred in her and her view that our organization lacked commitment to bold truths.

This was *very* difficult, and I know it was difficult and painful for my friend. I lost sleep in the days and weeks that I was replaying the situation in my head. My body felt the stress of longing for a good relationship and a commitment to work for lasting change. There were pieces of me that wanted to name that I was *right* to take the actions I had taken or to share the pain and stress this had caused me. I resisted the narratives that played in my mind and I did my best to practice the skills I had been learning, while also seeking the best path forward. We ultimately decided together that it would be most healing and transformative, and that it would achieve our hopes around doing racial equity work, to shift the program we had started under *our* organizational umbrella to the nonprofit she and a partner had started. We decided that we could pass along all the funding for the project she was leading to the new non-profit, and that we would provide support as a sponsor while they worked toward legal nonprofit status. We decided at that moment that placing a black woman in a role that limited her gifts, skills, and voice was not embodying the racial justice we sought to build. Simultaneously, we decided that I would continue to work to shift the culture of our organization and continue to navigate historic structures with hopes for mutual liberation.

Our friendship has continued to grow, and her voice continues to challenge me. I love her, and I believe she loves me. We love each other's children and families. At the same time, I am still not sure she fully *trusts* me, and I can understand why. We are trapped in centuries of systemic betrayal. Historical and current dynamics and cultures of racism are deeply embedded in our lives and relationships. Navigating these realities is a continual act of love. We live in an imperfect world in which mistakes have been made and will continue to be made. Rather than seeking a world free of mistakes or pain, I try to navigate with ways of life and love *in the midst* of it all.

Questions for Reflection

1. Recall a time you made a mistake when engaging in faith or political issues. How did you feel? Did you take action to correct the situation?

2. How do you recover from mistakes? How have you experienced connection amid relationship mistakes?

3. How does it feel to be "checked" in a constructive way by someone for whom you care?

4. What obstacles do you experience in being able to navigate mistakes?

Don't remember the prior things;

 don't ponder ancient history.

Look! I'm doing a new thing;

 now it sprouts up; don't you recognize it?

I'm making a way in the desert,

 paths in the wilderness.

The beasts of the field, the jackals and ostriches, will honor me,

 because I have put water in the desert

 and streams in the wilderness

 to give water to my people,

 my chosen ones.

— Isaiah 43:18–20, CEB

8

Cultivating Joy: Dance, Regardless

That day I was already tired as I drove to work. My exhaustion wasn't for any particular reason apart from the compounding lethargy that settles into our bones amid a too-full calendar. Call it compassion fatigue, or activism fatigue—all I knew was that I would rather lie on my couch than go anywhere. It was guilt that moved me out of my house and toward the work of the day. On my agenda was an invitation to speak at World Refugee Day. Wishing that I felt inspired, I settled for a sense of obligation and left my office to walk across the street to the Colorado State Capitol.

The sun shone on my face as I came closer to the sound of drums and singing. The smell of spicy stew and curry lifted my mood, and the energy of crowds of people in colorful clothing slowly revitalized my body. Recent refugees from countries all around the world had gathered on the plaza in front of the Colorado State Capitol steps with caretakers and advocates, city officials, and faith leaders, who were all chatting with one another, hugging, and laughing, each filled with joy simply to be together.

If I hadn't been paying attention to the daily news reports, I would have had no idea that the communities celebrating, eating, and singing and were under attack. During a global refugee crisis in which the greatest number of people since World War II were fleeing persecution or being forcibly removed from their homes, our government was not only turning its back but inciting hostility toward those seeking refuge. Images of a three-year-old boy washed up on shore, of a million people on foot moving in a caravan across Europe, or of overloaded boats filled with people fleeing for their lives did not soften the hearts of our leaders, who refused to welcome those in need, reversing long-held policies to support people in crisis.

Denying facts that show the net benefit our communities experience through welcoming refugees, our government cut numbers of immigrant admissions and support for immigrants and refugees in 2017, 2018, and 2019. Tens of thousands of people have died while our government frames policies that restrict criteria for welcome and cuts resources to support those seeking asylum. Refugees and immigrants are not only experiencing less opportunity and political legitimacy, but are feeling more discrimination, stereotyping, and acts of violence.

It was against this backdrop that I walked into a community that had come to celebrate. They had come to dance and sing and eat and share stories of survival and thriving amid overwhelming obstacles. By the time the celebration really got moving, my body was full and warm under the sun of a blazing Colorado June afternoon. The exhaustion and guilt I had felt driving to work had faded as I danced to the beat of the drums, laughing and bonding and in so doing laying the foundation for the critical work of advocacy and survival ahead. To this day, I feel an immediate sense of warmth and connection when I cross paths with anyone I met that day. Some people think celebration and joy are frivolous extras; I know they are acts of survival that keep us alive and moving forward.

* * * *

In the midst of the chaos of life, celebration, dance, and joy are countercultural practices that are important to cultivate. I have found that even a little moment of joy can provide the needed fuel to push through times of struggle and hopelessness. We each experience joy in our own way. I often feel deep joy as a result of slowing down, becoming aware of my breathing, and noticing the beauty of my surroundings. Joy takes me out of my head and into my heart to feel the connection to something beyond myself. Joy can be found in a planned celebration or can come in a mundane moment, but I must slow down to notice it. A posture of joy and celebration regardless of circumstances is revolutionary. In the long-haul work of building relationships across religious differences and fighting for political rights and equality, a posture of joy can help dismantle assumptions, tap into our shared humanity, and develop much-needed resilience for the inevitable struggles of living.

Joy in Religion

Resilient joy is not a new concept; instead, it is a piece of collective wisdom that has been passed on across religious traditions for thousands of years. Sacred texts speak of the human need to celebrate, and of the powerful feelings of love and connection that sustain us through difficulty and hardship. The word *joy* can be found nearly 200 times in the Bible (NRSV version), with about a quarter of those in the Psalms alone. Joy in the Bible is an emotion felt amid the real struggle and pain of living.

Similarly, the Qur'an and the Hadith, the teachings from the life of Mohamed, call for living life with joy. The concept of joy is woven throughout the sacred texts of the Upanishads, the Tao, and the Granth (the Sikh holy book). Across traditions, joy is found through our encounters with God and in our encounters with one another as we foster relationships and create lasting connection.

In Jewish tradition, *Shekhinah* is the face of God, the feminine "bride of the sabbath" who comes to sustain and shine light in the world. Shekhinah awakens our senses and energizes our body and mind and brings deep blessing; this "shining countenance" of God leads to a joy-filled life. Joy is an ultimate experience of *connection* with God, with one another, with nature and creation, and with body and soul, mind and spirit. This limitless well of joy inspires us to sing and dance, even amid suffering. The Psalms are overflowing with this joy:

> Let the heavens be glad, and let the earth rejoice;
>> let the sea roar, and all that fills it;
>> let the field exult, and everything in it.
> Then shall all the trees of the forest sing for joy
>> before the LORD; for he is coming,

for he is coming to judge the earth.

He will judge the world with righteousness,

and the people with his truth.

—Psalm 96:11–13

Clap your hands, all you peoples;

shout to God with loud songs of joy.

For the Lord, the Most High, is awesome,

a great king over all the earth.

He subdued peoples under us,

and nations under our feet.

—Psalm 47:1–3

My favorite book of the Bible—the Gospel of Luke—is woven together with themes of joy. The story begins with an unexpected pregnancy in old age as Zechariah and Elizabeth learn they will give birth to a child. An angel comes to Zechariah and promises that he will have "joy and gladness" at the birth of his son and that many will "rejoice" at his birth. In the next scene, Mary, pregnant with Jesus, greets her cousin Elizabeth, and the baby in Elizabeth's womb "leaped for joy." Mary exclaims, "My spirit rejoices in God." The whole earth shouts for joy with the birth of Christ as an angel calls out to the shepherds, "I am bringing you good news of great joy."

The opposite of joy in Jewish and Christian teachings is disconnection and depression. When we are hyper-focused on ourselves and our accomplishments, disconnected from God and from one another, we become isolated and fragmented. This is less dependent on specific circumstances and more about mindset—about focusing our mind on God and on our shared connection to one another. As someone who struggles with depression, I know my experience is compounded by the desire to disconnect and isolate that often comes alongside the tunnel vision of depression. Although mental health is more significant than merely changing a mindset, I see that my struggles are more intense when I am trapped in an inward, self-focused drive to "accomplish" rather than on an outward focus on seeing the face of God and celebrating life in the midst of struggle together. Reaching out for support or making myself vulnerable to another brings the joyful gratitude that I am not alone in the messiness of daily living. For me, this realization is the real root of joy.

Joy, regardless of circumstance, is the heart of eastern religions. In my early twenties, I began practicing meditation and studying the writings of the Upanishads and teachings of Buddhism. Through these teachings and practices, I learned about the core Buddhist teaching that suffering and joy are two sides of the same coin. Of course, we should still confront oppression, but we can do so from a place of calm confidence rather than anxious frenzy. Seeing suffering for what it is, the inevitable reality of life strips away the pain of its control over our well-being. Seeking the place within that is beyond suffering leads to a feeling of deep joy. For me, this invited both my continued action to work for justice in the world and a sincere acknowledgment that I cannot control the world. Pain and suffering are built into the fabric of life. If I can acknowledge that at the deepest level, I can continue to work for shared well-being here and now with less dependence on seeing an immediate result from my efforts. Although this may seem counter-intuitive, for me it has been a truth beyond words. Joy in the midst of suffering and pain is a deep source of resilience.

Revolutionary Joy

For the Palestinian people, no pain is more profound than the loss of their land and homes. The impact of the 1948 *Nakba,* or "catastrophe," when 700,000 Palestinians were forced to flee their homes, continues to be felt in families and communities who to this day fight for survival. Amid decades of violence, heartbreak, and political strife, traditional folkloric *dabke* dancing provides a subversive path for creative protest and joy. Dabke is an Arabic folk dance that originated in the mountainous regions above the Mediterranean coastline and the Tigris River. Long ago, people of the villages and towns of Lebanon, Syria, Palestine, Jordan, Iraq, and some Quasi-Bedouin tribes that were in nearby territories all danced the dabke.

Historically, houses in these regions were built with mud and tree branches, and with changes in the weather sometimes these would crack. Members of the family and wider community would come and patch up the cracks, forming a line, joining hands, and stomping the new mud into place. In colder months, they would sing to stay warm.

Even when technological developments improved roofs and made the communal repair ritual unnecessary, the tradition of the dance and song continued as a reminder of the importance of family, community, and solidarity. Today, dabke is used as an act of protest or to express resilience in the face of violence and oppression. Though their land may be taken and their dignity may be threatened, for the Palestinians joy, community, and dancing cannot be contained. Coming together, locking arms, stomping the ground, and singing in unison stirs feelings of empathy, strength, and determination. Although the dabke originated from a necessary act of repairing a neighbor's roof or walls, it has now become a symbol of life, love, and struggle.

Hallelujah Anyhow

For black churches in America, cultivating joy is a matter of survival. Navigating racism, pain, and violence were not new for black churches in America, or for Mother Emanuel AME when on the evening of June 17, 2015, a young man shot and killed nine people praying in their church basement during a Wednesday night Bible study. The horrific act of violence shocked the country and brought to light the deep hatred and racism that persist in this country. Mother Emanuel Church has a two hundred-year history of building resilience in the face of oppression and hatred. The AME Church itself was born out of a desire for true freedom and liberation from slavery and the continued segregation and discrimination that persisted in the church. Black churches were and continue to be places of refuge, celebration, and joy amid a society that has long rejected and harmed black people. This joy does not dismiss righteous anger or pass over the need for real repair and justice. Rather, it fosters resilience and strength.

Following the horrific murders on that terrible Wednesday night, the people of Mother Emanuel navigated the pain as best they could. In an article in the *New Yorker* a few months after the tragedy, Mother Emanuel pastor Norvel Goff Sr., names the ways in which the church is surviving with prayers, the encouragement of the community, and the guidance of God.[1] He speaks of the ways in

---

[1]David Remnick, "Blood at the Root: In the aftermath of the Emanuel Nine," *The New Yorker* (Sept. 21, 2015). Available at https://www.newyorker.com/magazine/2015/09/28/blood-at-the-root.

which the community continues to find *joy* amid the suffering. He makes a clear distinction between the common spiritual condition of "joy"—an intense awareness of the gift of life, the fruit of hope, joy as the very condition of being alive—and the banality of "happiness." There was no happiness, he says. But "even in the midst of trials and tribulations, we still have joy." Goff says that "while members of the community were in a state of immense pain, they were alive, and feeling joy in their pews—and at their jobs, and at their Bible classes and dinner tables and Sunday strolls—because of the depth of their spiritual lives."

For Mother Emanuel AME Church, this is the way of being that has been engrained since the days when enslaved black people, in a quest for safety, community, dignity, cohesion, empowerment, ritual, and peace, broke from white churches and built "invisible" institutions, sometimes called "hush harbors." The Mother Emanuel AME Church, even as it has changed, aged, and, in some places, lost ground to mega-churches, remains a central institution of black life, and of black political influence.

▼ ....

During the time of slavery, enslaved African people developed songs called spirituals. The songs grew organically and were passed on with no written lyrics. Now as then, the songs preserve culture, pass on knowledge—often including coded knowledge—and build strength and resilience in the midst of horrific circumstances. From "Lift Every Voice and Sing" to "We Shall Overcome", song carries people through and builds strength and resilience.

.... ◢

Say It Clear, Say It Loud. Gay Is Good, Gay Is Proud

For the GLBTQ community, resilient and resistant joy have been the keys to personal strength and political recognition. In 1969, "homosexual acts" such as kissing, holding hands, or dancing together were illegal in the United States. Not only were LGBTQ people marginalized, they were at constant risk of personal and institutional violence. One of the few places in which LGBTQ persons felt free and safe was in the sanctuary of underground gay bars and nightclubs. However, police regularly raided gay nightclubs, arresting people who were wearing clothing that didn't conform to their assigned gender or those they suspected of "soliciting" same sex relations. Until 1966, bars in New York could be punished or even shut down for serving alcohol to LGBTQ people. Stonewall Inn was one of the few bars that defiantly welcomed LGBTQ people and drag queens.

On the night of June 28, 1969, police raided the Stonewall Inn in New York and started arresting bar patrons and employees who were violating the law about gender-appropriate clothing. When an officer clubbed black lesbian Stormé DeLarverie over the head for complaining that her handcuffs were too tight, the crowd had had enough: They actively resisted the police by throwing bricks, bottles, and shot glasses. Police officers took sledgehammers to the jukebox and the cigarette machine and "confiscated" the cash register. Bar patrons then formed dance lines to taunt police officers and chanted words like "Fag power" and "Liberate the bar." The *NY Daily News* reported at the time that thirteen people were arrested and three police officers were injured on the first night of what would become a week-long protest.[2]

In the days that followed, for the first time queer and trans people demanded that their human dignity be seen and respected. Fred Sargeant, a man who attended the events, wrote that there were "no floats, no music, no boys in briefs." Instead, they held signs and banners and chanted, "Say it clear, say it loud. Gay is good, gay is proud." The Stonewall Riot is credited as the start of the modern LGBTQ rights movement. Quite different from the Pride parades of today, the six days of queer folx marching in the streets was the beginning of a long tradition of queer resistance through parades, singing, and dancing. Among this community, too, persistent joy was and is a primary way of expressing resilience and resistance, as well as living into full joy and humanity in the face of hate, bigotry, and violence.

* * * *

Collective joy can be powerfully subversive. Liberation movements have a long history of nurturing and employing joy through song, dance, celebration, ritual, and cultivating

---

[2]"Stonewall Inn is raided by police in 1969," *New York Daily News* (June 23, 2015), reprint of an article by Dennis Eskew published in the *New York Daily News* on June 29, 1969. Available at https://www.nydailynews.com/new-york/stonewall-riot-place-1969-article-1.2267954.

mindfulness. In her book *Dancing in the Streets,* writer Barbara Ehrenreich argues that collective dancing is a nearly universal "biotechnology" for binding groups together.[3] Remember the flash mob craze of a few years ago? Physical movement releases emotion and creates bonding, trust, and equality. Moving together dissolves hierarchies and increases a sense of community. The power of shared movement literally helps us survive. Human beings have survived due to our ability to coordinate, cooperate, and build a robust community with other groups. Historically, the ability to create group cohesion through dance and other bonding methods gave certain groups an advantage over those that did not.

Yet our culture tends to emphasize individual accomplishments, competition, and privatization. This hyper-individualized way of moving through the world leads to isolation, loneliness, and division. Collective joy is a countercultural reclamation of our inherent connection to one another and a dominant force in bringing people together, claiming our shared humanity, and building strength to work for personal and political inclusion and thriving. There is something about dance, celebration, and resilient joy that disrupts tension and channels it into inspiring and sustaining energy.

* * * *

Perennial Joy

The King of Death:

The joy of the spirit ever abides,

But not what seems pleasant to the senses.

Both these, differing in their purpose, prompt us

To action. All is well for those who choose

The joy of the spirit, but they miss

The goal of life who prefer the pleasant.

Perennial joy or passing pleasure?

This is the choice one is to make always.

---

[3] Barbara Ehrenreich, *Dancing in the Streets: A History of Collective Joy* (New York: Metropolitan Books, 2007).

The wise recognize this, but not

The ignorant. The first welcome what leads to joy

Abiding, even though painful at the time.

The latter run, goaded by their senses,

After what seems immediate pleasure.

Well have you renounced these passing pleasures

So dear to the senses, Nachiketa,

And turned your back on the way of the world

Which makes mankind forget the goal of life.

Far apart are wisdom and ignorance:

The first leads one to Self-realization;

The second makes one more and more

Estranged from one's real Self. I regard you,

Nachiketa, as worthy of instruction,

For passing pleasures tempt you not at all.

—from *The Katha Upanishad* (trans. Eknath Easwaran)

Joy as a Political Act

When we experience and cultivate innate joy, we realize that we are not alone. We begin to see that joy resides in each of us and that part of our human experience is a call to joy. The cultivation of unconditional joy taps into our underlying capacity for freedom and interconnectedness. Realizing this, we come to see and treat one another in response to our inherent light. In my experience, one of the most significant ways to break down stereotypes and assumptions and to see the divine in one another is through laughing, singing, dancing, and celebrating together. Experiencing this level of connection amid pain and struggle creates a bond that is beyond words. For me, this leads to a practical joy that inspires us to imagine the world as it could be and provides the fuel to take real steps to move toward that world.

It may feel selfish take time to celebrate and experience joy amid a political climate that has life-and-death consequences for so many. This is why joy is a political act. Choosing joy over fear, division, fragmentation, and hyper-competition means resisting the forces that oppress. Connecting with one another and nurturing our inner joy is a matter of survival. When we see how contagious and powerful joy is, we experience the solidarity and resilience that is necessary to build long-term systemic transformation. When we acknowledge that suffering is inevitable but need not control us, we find freedom.

We all know that our current political climate is toxic. We are seeing diminishing human rights, walls instead of bridges, and the use of old tropes to scapegoat and demonize people. Common decency and shared values rooted in respect and kindness have fallen by the wayside. In my work in our Colorado state legislature, I have seen less bipartisan agreement to work for change around our shared struggles. Yet I have also witnessed breakthroughs when we take the time to step back from our divisions and be together to celebrate or mourn. I have stood together on stage and at vigils with people with radically different political views, all of us committed to speaking up against violence and division. In such moments, we know that we are together for something that is bigger than our divisions. That joyful commitment grounds us and helps us celebrate our shared humanity regardless of our different views or our painful past. Creating space for joy and connection can lead to seeing the humanity in those with whom we may vehemently disagree. Cultivating joy holds revolutionary political potential.

Cultivating Joy

Joy is a posture, a practice, a way of being that can be cultivated. It is also always fleeting, making the work of cultivating joy a lifelong pursuit. I once asked a mentor how I could possibly *find balance* as a mom attending seminary. She wisely exclaimed, "You will never *find* balance. You will always *navigate* it, no matter what you have going on, but you will never *find* it." The same is true of cultivating joy. Deep joy is not naive or based on whim, but comes from the internal well within each of us. By intentionally developing joy in our internal state of being, as well as in our communities, we build endurance for the long-haul work of loving and working for justice in our convoluted worlds of faith and politics.

Though the path to joy is different for each of us, there are common practices that can help us connect to the inner source of abundant joy. Cultivating joy entails a return to God and to one another. It entails moving beyond fear and doubt and moving toward genuine delight. By cultivating joy in less complicated spaces, we will more easily find joy in difficult and painful spaces. What follows are some suggestions for how to cultivate this joy.

Slow Down

1. *Take time to practice gratitude.* It seems this has become a cliché, but it works. Often our critical side wins in the battle for brain space. Practicing gratitude intentionally tells the critical side to step back while we create space for appreciation. This not only changes our brain patterns but can shift our relationships and interactions with others.

2. *Grow something.* Whether it be a plant, a fish, a garden, animals, or the young people in our lives, when we take time to nurture, care, and cultivate life, we move outside of our own internal dramas and notice the ways life is continuously moving and changing. Actually watch plants, soil, children, and animals, and see the life force moving in them, independent of you. Feel deep joy flood your body as you wonder at life.

3. *People watch.* When I am feeling down, I sometimes go to a crowded space like a coffee shop or a downtown corner or an airport and people watch. I imagine what each person was like as a child. I wonder about the loves in their lives and the ways in which they struggle. I send them loving-kindness with my gaze and my energy. I find that sending out this love to strangers expands love and joy within me and between us. Sending loving energy to strangers changes the loop tape of criticism and judgment that I have about myself and others.

Fill Up

1. *Read sacred texts from your own tradition and others.* I am continually baffled that people universally have been experiencing the emotions of love, pain, and joy across

centuries and across cultures. Reading the Bible or the Qur'an or the Upanishads sparks curiosity and imagination and reminds us that we are not alone in this wild experience of being human and seeking to live our lives well. Beyond traditional sacred texts, take time to read classic texts of spirituality and justice. Read bell hooks or Zora Neal Hurston. The words of twentieth-century Jesuit priest, paleontologist, and geologist Pierre Teilhard de Chardin move in my soul. Annie Dillard makes me laugh out loud and cry simultaneously. What fills your soul? How do words from those who have walked before us make you feel connected? Take time to explore words of the past and to sit with stories of joyful resilience in the lives of those who have walked these paths before.

2. *Watch a movie that makes you laugh.* Stories have power. Even stories and films that seem simple or "mindless" can shift our ways of moving through the world. When life is heavy, I watch a movie that is guaranteed to make me laugh, such as *Tommy Boy* or *Bridesmaids*. Neither of these movies will shape my views on justice, but they will lighten my spirit and help me get up the next day and continue the heavy heart-and-mind work of seeking mutual liberation. Sometimes we need laughter and a break from the hard work to be able to stick with it for the long haul.

3. *Listen to music.* Music can speak to a piece of ourselves that is unreachable in any other way. Music can spark memories or evoke imagination and can root us in something bigger than ourselves. For me, few things are better than rolling down the car windows on a beautiful day and turning up my favorite song. Besides that, one of my favorite places is our local outdoor music venue, Red Rocks Amphitheater. Being in nature and among a crowd of ten thousand people singing and moving together stirs my soul as not much else can. Take time to let your favorite music move you.

Get out

1. *Serve.* We all know it is better to give than to receive. Stepping out of my regular routine to make sandwiches with people living on the street or to help a neighbor with her yard work has

a way of shaking me out of any funk and into more profound joy. It reminds me that we need one another. Taking time to help others also reminds me that it is ok to ask for and receive support when I need it.

2. *Move your body!* One of my family's greatest gifts is our connection with the Filipino American Cultural Center in Denver. In Filipino communities such as this, dance is integrated into every single gathering. We dance at Christmas parties, Valentine's Day parties, summer celebrations, and even Thanksgiving dinner celebrations. Through moving our bodies we feel connected to one another, we are more humble (if you saw my dance moves, you would know why), and we laugh a lot. Find a place where you can move your body and be carefree.

3. *Step into nature.* Getting outside—breathing fresh air, taking time to observe trees and birds and soil—reminds us how big the world is and puts all of life into perspective. Seeing trees change and shed leaves in the fall, watching the dormant space of winter, and observing the new life of spring remind us of the cycles of life and the ebb and flow of death. Joy can be found in watching the remarkable movements of inchworms or blue herons and being reminded of our own capacities and place in the world.

Joy Meditation

Here is a simple meditation that can be done in eight breaths, or longer if you have more time. Each breath has a single word to help you remember how to focus your attention.

Find a comfortable place to sit. Drop into your body with kindness and feel what's arising. Feel your face come into a gentle smile. Listen to the sounds that greet you. Feel your connection to all that surrounds you.

1. With the first breath, bring your awareness to the sensation of your breathing. Pay attention to your body and your breath

as it moves in and out. Feel the push of your belly and the rise of your chest. Follow your in-breath and out-breath from beginning to end. Silently say the word *breath*.

2. With the second breath, bring your attention to the fullness of your body, from your toes to your legs, hips, stomach, chest, arms, shoulders, throat, to the top of your head. Allow your awareness to fill your body completely, and notice what you find. Feel and observe each sensation as it arises without trying to change it. Silently say the word *body*.

3. With the third breath, notice any tension in your body and exhale to release any heaviness or agitation. Imagine yourself as a dishrag being rinsed and wrung out by your breath. Silently say the word *release*.

4. With the fourth breath, inhale and say to yourself, "May you have ease and lightness of body and mind." Focus on your heart and fill yourself with love and generosity toward yourself. Send yourself compassion, kindness, and grace. Silently say the word *love*.

5. With the fifth breath, notice any longings or aversions that arise. Is there any part of you that wants reality to be different than it is right now? Is there a sense in which you are fighting against things-as-they-are? Notice any of these longings and aversions and let yourself feel them without passing judgment or trying to make them go away. Silently say the word *longing*.

6. With the sixth breath, become aware that everything you need is already present in this moment. You have everything you need to experience peace, joy, and freedom. Although you have infinite reasons to suffer and are by nature vulnerable, you can tap into our communal power here and now. Pain and suffering do exist, but they are not all that exists. Breathe out the inevitable brokenness. Silently say the phrase *let go*.

7. With the seventh breath, become aware that you are alive. As you breathe, feel the energy of life moving through you.

Recognize the miracle of being alive. Focus on everything in life that is present and whole. Silently say the word *alive*.

8. With the eighth breath, become aware of all of the feelings of joy within and around you. As soon as we let go of our desires and wake up to the present moment, we see that reality itself is indescribably beautiful. All of our senses—our sight, sound, smell, taste, touch, and mental perception—deliver this beauty to us like a precious gift. All we have to do is enjoy it. Silently say the word *joy*.

We can practice the eight breaths to joy like this:

- Breath (in/out)

- Body (in/out)

- Release (in/out)

- Love (in/out)

- Longing (in/out)

- Let go (in/out)

- Alive (in/out)

- Joy (in/out)

The Face of God in One Another

I walked into the great hall at the Parliament of World Religions in Salt Lake City, took off my shoes, picked up a blue scarf for my head, and made my way into my first *langar*. Langar (rhymes with hunger) means "kitchen," after the community kitchen in every *gurdwara*, or Sikh house of worship, around the world. Langar is a free meal served to anyone in the community without distinction of race, religion, class, gender, or economic or social status. Everyone, all around the world, sits on the floor side by side as equals and is served a vegetarian meal prepared and served by volunteers. A tradition started in India in the sixteenth century by the founder of Sikhism, Guru Nanak, langar was both a political statement claiming the equality of all people and a practical way of honoring our most profound connection and human need to eat. Today millions of people eat together in gurdwaras around the world; nearly a hundred thousand people eat each day at the Golden Temple in Amritsar, India. They eat free of charge, connected by our collective human needs for food and community.

When people think about religion, they often think about our divisions and the many wars that have been fought in the name of religion. We think about dogma and hypocrisy and different theories and ideologies about God and the universe and heaven and hell. The Parliament of World Religions was launched in the late nineteenth century to counter such religious divisions and build unity and power to influence the common good. On this day at the Parliament, six thousand people would be fed by volunteers in the great hall of Salt Lake City's convention center. I walked into a rainbow of red, blue, yellow, green, and orange headscarves. People in monk robes, preacher suits, priest collars, turbans, kippahs, and everything in between all sat on the floor in rows. In this space there are no divisions; we all sit on the floor side by side. I wound my way through the line, was handed a tray, and was guided to sit down in a row. Pairs of people wearing traditional turbans and *bana* (Sikh spiritual attire) walked along the rows and scooped dal and then rice and beans from a large pot held by a friend onto each plate along with a piece of chapati. Another set of young people came by and handed cups of warm chai to each of us. I took a breath and looked around in awe of the beauty of the moment. What if the world were more like *this*? I took a few bites of the delicious food and talked with my neighbors sitting on the floor cross-legged by my side. We asked one another where we were from, what had brought us to the Parliament, what we thought so far. We smiled and laughed, we inhaled with gratitude, and we ate.

The feeling of connection was beyond words. We glimpsed a world that was more than our divisions and pettiness. That was as nourishing for the soul as the food on our plates was for our bodies. It was an experience of joy.

For me, it is such moments that sustain and pull me to keep moving forward. Joy is more significant than basic happiness and fun—although these contribute to joy. Joy is a feeling that surpasses conditions and painful contexts and settles into our bones with a sense of real peace. I experience this joy when I am sitting around a table with friends and loved ones sharing stories, drinking a glass of wine, and laughing. Or when I am running on the trail near the river by my house, watching a blue heron waiting patiently for fish to come near the surface of the water, and observing Cooper's hawks soar and dive for food to feed their babies on a beautiful sunny day. I even feel this joy when I am at work, thinking through how we will respond to the latest community need in a way that will weave us together and bring healing, and someone cracks a joke and we all roar in laughter. Or when I walk across the street from my office and bump into familiar legislators and people who work at the State Capitol, I feel joy when we stop and hug and catch up even briefly on each other's children or health, or commiserate about the latest drama we are navigating.

Oddly enough, each of these are moments when I feel deep joy. There is joy in understanding that we are all connected. We are in this together. We care about one another. *We even love one another.* We are committed to working each day, in the midst of it all, to build communities where all can thrive.

"The Guest House"

This being human is a guest house.

Every morning a new arrival.

A joy, a depression, a meanness,

some momentary awareness comes

as an unexpected visitor.

Welcome and entertain them all!

Even if they are a crowd of sorrows,

who violently sweep your house

empty of its furniture,

still, treat each guest honorably.

He may be clearing you out

for some new delight.

The dark thought, the shame, the malice,

meet them at the door laughing and invite them in.

Be grateful for whatever comes,

because each has been sent

as a guide from beyond.

—Rumi

Questions for Reflection

1. In interfaith work, there is a concept called *holy envy*. This is the idea that there are things in traditions different from our own that we appreciate and admire. Is there something about a religious tradition that is not your own that you appreciate, admire, even envy? Is there something about the "other" political party you admire?

2. How does it feel to experience joy with someone with whose faith or politics you profoundly disagree?

3. How does joy move in your body?

4. Have you ever embraced joy in the midst of pain?

9

Letting Go, Holding On:
What About My Family?

In the midst of the 2016 election, I was concerned that recovering from such a divisive election season would be hard on our community. While I was confident that "my side" would win in the end, I was genuinely worried about the backlash that would come from Trump supporters when he lost. I wondered how we would put the pieces back together after a campaign season filled with such vitriol. In my concern, I reached out to leaders from three local universities with different religious and political outlooks to build a program called "Healing Our Divides." We brought together conservative Evangelical people connected to Denver Seminary, liberal Protestant Christian people from Iliff School of Theology, and people from the Catholic community at the Institute for Common Good at Regis University, a Jesuit university.

We held a series of dialogues engaging in "real dialogue across real difference." Rather than shying away from hot political issues, we stepped into the fire and sought to do so in ways that encourage listening and respect. Our goals were not to come to any sort of agreement or to become friends and head to brunch together. Instead, we sought to see the basic humanity in one another beyond the caricatures and to build a desire to refrain from hurting one another. We launched headfirst into topics such as religious freedom, gender and sexuality, and poverty and the role of the government.

At the first event, I watched as people started to fill the large conference room at Regis University. Some were familiar, others not. I was cautiously intrigued. I knew enough people in the room to realize there could be some contentious conversations. I noticed an editor of a local conservative Catholic newspaper sit down next to the director of the Colorado Religious Coalition for Reproductive Choice, and I said a little prayer that our plan would not backfire. My stress was unfounded. In fact, the two engaged in thoughtful conversation with honesty about their perspectives and treated each other with kindness and respect. We learned from each conversation, planted seeds of understanding, and tweaked the program and format in anticipation of future events.

The day after one of these events, I gathered with our monthly rabbi and clergy study group. Several group members had been at the Healing Our Divides event the previous night. As people were telling stories from their experience, one of my rabbi friends, an older man who had been rabbi of our largest local synagogue and whose wife had served as a state senator, chimed in and said, "What a waste of time." Intrigued, and always happy for feedback, I leaned in and said, "Tell me more!" He said, "I have no desire to spend any more time with *those* people. I would rather focus my energy on building up *my* people to win."

The words struck me and continue to reverberate even today. Surely we must do "both/and." Surely we must build up those who are working for rights, equality, and a more just country for *all people*. And, if we are to find long-term transformation and mutual liberation, we must also reach out and continue to reach out, even across political differences.

I continue to wrestle with the question of when to let go of an effort to build a relationship across our differences, and when to hold on. When should we commit our time and energy to try to connect with someone who may hold beliefs or values that demean and dehumanize others? When should we prioritize preserving our own health, well-being, and precious energy to build up our own community and gain power and skills to "win" votes or public opinion? When should we open our arms with loving-kindness?

Should we set a clear boundary and protect our well-being or the well-being of others? How much time and energy should we spend engaging in conflicts over religion and politics with family and loved ones? When are these conversations vital to the work of long-term transformation, and when do they do more harm than good?

In the middle of our Healing Our Divides series, the election of November 2016 brought to light just how deep the divides were. "My side" did not win, and there was no end in sight for the vitriol that had opened so many wounds. We had an event scheduled for November 10, 2016, two days after the election. We changed the planned agenda to process the results of the election and invited both people who were happy with the results and those who were not. That those who were unhappy were far more comfortable speaking publicly, and those who had voted for Trump did not feel comfortable speaking up in the space we had provided. This exemplified the ongoing difficulty of engaging in this work. We realized amid this gathering that our subconscious intent in starting this program had been to assure we could rebuild our community after we won. After the election, we realized that the dis-ease in society was much more significant, and the need for healing was far more pressing than who "won" and who "lost." We were challenged to enter into contentious spaces and decide where to spend our time and energy daily.

* * * *

How do we discern when to set a boundary and *let go* of efforts to bridge a divide in religion and politics? When do we open ourselves to *hold on* and seek deeper relationships across our vast differences? Our faith traditions have the wisdom to guide us in these critical questions. I learned from my friend Rabbi Brian that medieval kabbalists (Jewish mystics) believed that God cannot be fully understood, but has been revealed in attributes that interact with each other and with the world. Just as we each have internal traits that make up our personalities and guide our ways of moving through the world, so too does God. Kabbalists name and understand these ten traits through the figure of the *sefirot,* sometimes called the tree of life.

The ten traits of the sefirot represent parts of God and parts of us. Understanding God helps us understand ourselves. These different parts provide us with the balance to move through the world in ways that bring healing and justice. The book *Essential Judaism: A Complete Guide to Beliefs, Customs & Rituals,* names the ten attributes of God as *Keter* (Crown), *Hokhmah* (Wisdom), *Binah* (Understanding), *Hesed* (Lovingkindness), *Gevurah* (Might) or *Din* (Judgment), *Tiferet* (Beauty), *Hod* (Splendor), *Netzah* (Victory), *Yesod* (Foundation), *Malkhut* (Sovereignty) or *Shekhinah* (the Divine Presence), and *Da'at* (Knowledge), where all ten of the sefirot are united as one.[1] Each of the attributes represents one aspect of God, and each element is identified with a part of the body.

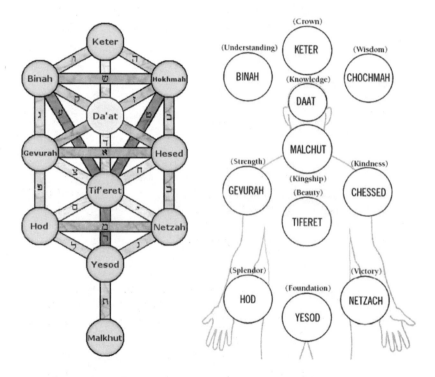

The right side of the body, most clearly seen in Gevurah, is the side of judgment, limitation, strength, and discipline. The right side evokes the awe or fear of God and provides boundaries, accountability, and structure in our lives. It is often called "might" because it represents God's absolute power. Gevurah is associated with the ability to restrain goodness when that goodness would

---

[1]George Robinson, *Essential Judaism: A Complete Guide to Beliefs, Customs & Rituals* (New York: Atria Books, 2000).

be misused or would allow others to be hurt. Gevurah (might) counterbalances Chessed (or Hesed).

The left side, exemplified in Chessed, is the side of unconditional loving-kindness. In Jewish theology, Chessed is like God's love for the children of Israel. This love spills out and promotes love between people. Chessed is a virtue that brings love and mercy from God toward humanity and contributes toward tikkun olam (repairing the world). Chessed represents the generous, open, benevolent side of God and is evidenced in grace and compassion. Chessed is often the founding principle in Jewish ethics and is the source of connection above and beyond any expectations. Chessed draws us into relationships.

To have balance and justice, and to thrive, we must have both the right arm of Gevurah providing strength, boundaries, and judgment, and the left arm of Chessed providing openness, unconditional love, and compassion. Kabbalah teaches that without the boundaries of Gevurah, the world would be so overwhelmed by God's love that it would be absorbed into God. Without the unconditional love of Chessed, God's judgment would unleash forces of destruction on the world. We need a balance of justice and mercy from God and in our own relationships. Our task is to find this balance.

An example of this can be found in Genesis 18, a central text of the Hebrew Bible, as Abraham challenges God to show mercy in the face of the judgment of the towns of Sodom and Gomorrah.

The people of Sodom and Gomorrah are known for their wicked ways, *not homosexuality*, as is so often declared, but corruption, lack of hospitality, and use of power to rape and oppress the vulnerable. God is fed up and sends angels to scope out the situation. Upon learning about God's plans, Abraham boldly petitions God to show mercy. The two negotiate: Abraham asks God to refrain from the destruction of the towns if fifty righteous people can be found there. When God agrees, Abraham continues to push, until they agree that God will have mercy if even ten righteous people can be found. The boundary is set at ten. When ten people cannot be found, Sodom and Gomorrah are destroyed in a rain of fiery sulfur. Abraham's nephew Lot and his daughters are spared, though Lot's wife is turned into a pillar of salt for disobeying by looking back longingly toward her home.

The story of Sodom and Gomorrah exemplifies the wrath and mercy, law and grace, boundaries and openness that we each negotiate daily. This is *not* a text about a standard of moral purity aligned with our current notions. (The second half of chapter 19 exposes that this text is not "God's little instruction book" with direct correlation to our lives today—this is where Lot's daughters get him drunk and sleep with him one by one in an effort to carry on the family name.) The text *does* invite us to explore important questions about how we discern whether relationships and situations are redeemable or irredeemable and how we negotiate boundaries and freedom. What is our boundary line? What are our core values that determine our willingness to stay in or leave a relationship? What limits do we maintain as we engage in the work of religion and politics?

The Christian scripture Matthew 10:12–15 cites the story of Sodom and Gomorrah when Jesus instructs his disciples on how to navigate rejection and persecution as they work for radical love, healing, and social transformation. Jesus tells his disciples that he is sending them out like sheep to the wolves. He warns them that the path will be steep. That they are following the teachings of the Rabbi Jesus means they are challenging religious assumptions of the day and calling for a countercultural revolution that imagines a new social order. In the disciples' world, moral authority is based not on one's pedigree or mindless adherence to legalistic piety, but on the health, well-being, and thriving of the people. As Mary proclaimed, the rich are poor, the hungry are fed, and the sick are healed. This message will surely stir things up and evoke strong reactions from those who have the ears to hear.

Jesus warns his disciples that this message may put them in harm's way. In fact, says Jesus, the followers should expect to be dragged before kings and governors and flogged for what they will say. Yet he tells them that they should not be discouraged by such persecution and lack of welcome. Instead, they should "shake the dust from their feet as they leave the house or town." Those who reject the message, says Jesus, "will be treated worse than those from the land of Sodom and Gomorrah on the day of judgment." He is not done. He continues:

"Do not think that I have come to bring peace to the earth;
I have not come to bring peace, but a sword.

For I have come to set a man against his father,
and a daughter against her mother,
and a daughter-in-law against her mother-in-law;
and one's foes will be members of one's own
household.

Whoever loves father or mother more than me is not
worthy of me; and whoever loves son or daughter more
than me is not worthy of me; and whoever does not take
up the cross and follow me is not worthy of me. Those who
find their life will lose it, and those who lose their life for
my sake will find it. "Whoever welcomes you welcomes
me, and whoever welcomes me welcomes the one who sent
me. Whoever welcomes a prophet in the name of a prophet
will receive a prophet's reward; and whoever welcomes a
righteous person in the name of a righteous person will
receive the reward of the righteous; and whoever gives
even a cup of cold water to one of these little ones in the
name of a disciple—truly I tell you, none of these will lose
their reward." (Matthew 10:34–42)

In this text, we see that following the higher laws of radical
love and inclusion leads to a revolutionary new social order but will
bring division in families. Those who prioritize the status quo and
traditional power structures will reject a message of social justice.
Jesus goes on to say that although they will experience strife, it
will be in the name of righteousness. A more profound way of life
is found in living the law of love and justice. The accurate measure
of righteousness is in the one who gives even a cup of cold water
to a little one.

The boundaries set by Jesus in this text, and by God in
the story of Sodom and Gomorrah, must be seen as going
hand in hand with stories of radical love and inclusion found
throughout the Hebrew and christian scriptures. While God's
right arm provides a boundary, God's left arm pulls people in.
In text after text throughout the Hebrew scriptures, the people
of Israel make incredible mistakes and can't seem to follow even
the most basic rules. After escaping slavery in Egypt, the people
follow Moses to the foot of Mount Sinai, where they receive the
Ten Commandments with clear instructions. Within forty days
they have broken nearly every one of them. In response, Moses

pleads for God's mercy toward the people. God responds that he is "The LORD, the LORD, a God merciful and gracious, slow to anger, and abounding in steadfast love and faithfulness, keeping steadfast love for the thousandth generation" (Exodus 34:6–7). In the christian scriptures, Jesus exemplifies mercy and loving-kindness when challenged by the Canaanite woman to heal her daughter, even though the disciples ask Jesus to send her away.

The Chinese philosophy principle of yin and yang from the third century B.C.E. states that all things exist as inseparable and contradictory opposites. The yin yang symbol signifies how the two opposites attract and complement each other, with each side having at its core an element of the other (represented by the small dots). Both poles are equal to the other and work in synchrony to maintain balance and order. As expressed in the *I Ching*, the ever-changing relationship between the two poles is responsible for the constant flux of the universe, and of life in general. When there is too high an imbalance between yin and yang, catastrophes occur. In ways similar to the balance of order in the sefirot of Kabbalah, we can see that life is grounded on a balance and rhythm that pulls us close and pushes us away in a continual effort to achieve equanimity.

* * * *

So what does this all have to do with navigating contentious spaces of relationships at the intersection of religion and politics? My experience is that these spaces are a constant push and pull. One needs discernment and wisdom to know when to open up and when to draw a line. Simple answers and inflexible ideology fall flat. Some issues are complicated, and often there are multiple ways to view the same situation. Although we should be able to articulate our values, the reality is that we will encounter experiences where our own deeply held values wind up in competition. For example, I prioritize my family relationships. I love and respect my family. They are good people caring for those in need in their communities, and some of them have different political views than I do. There are views that people in my family hold that I experience as hurtful (even if unintentional), or that I know hurt people I care about. How do we navigate family relationships with people who hold views that are at odds with what we hold most dear? I believe that in these moments it is good to step back and ask:

- What are my boundaries?

- What specific issues are most important to me?

- What core values drive my decisions?

- If I need to confront a friend or family member who is degrading and dehumanizing another person, *how* will I do that?

- When do I walk away from a person or situation? Is it possible to walk away in love?

- When do I maintain a relationship even if I am challenged by deep disagreements?

- What value system drives this decision?

- Who is affected by my decisions to stay in a difficult situation?

- Whose side am I on?

* * * *

Where Are the Fundamentalists?

One of the most frequent questions I receive when doing interfaith work is, "Where are the fundamentalists?" Quite often, those who show up and who are interested in engaging in work across religious and political differences are more progressive, moderate, or independent. Rarely do people from the farthest right end of the religious or political spectrum show up to do bridging work. I am sure there are many reasons for this, including perhaps a feeling of being judged or of not feeling safe sharing oppositional viewpoints. I find it challenging to engage in bridging work with people who hold hyper-exclusive or purist views. There is very little I can do if a person or group believes their way is the only way and that those who hold other views are less than human or condemned to hell. Or if someone believes they are personally at risk if they associate with people who hold differing views. As Robert Jones Jr. (@SonofBaldwin) said, "We can disagree and still love each other unless your disagreement is rooted in my oppression and denial of my humanity and right to exist."[2]

Certainly, there are people who experience revolutionary transformation or let go of extremist or fundamentalist views. But they are uncommon. Certainly, there are people who have escaped the Islamic extremism of ISIS, or who have been de-radicalized and become free from white supremacist groups. The move away from extremism, radicalism, or fundamentalism of any kind is a big leap. Those who change their fundamentalist views often experience intense disorientation and severe backlash from their own communities, as did my friend Rob Schenck. I met Rob at a Bridging Divides workshop in 2018 in New York City where we connected immediately. When Rob learned that I had grown up in Colorado Springs just down the street from Focus on the Family, he told me that he had spent many years working in coalitions with the Religious Right and that we likely knew some of the same people.

Rob was a founder of the extremist anti-abortion movement of the 1980s through 2010. He masterminded the tactic of using an actual aborted fetus as a prop at rallies and was arrested after handing the fetus to President Bill Clinton at the 1992 Democratic National Convention. Rob's story has been presented in the Netflix movie *The Armor of Light*,[3] and he has written a book, *Costly Grace*.[4] Although I would not have been able to be friends with the Rob portrayed in the movie and the book, the Rob I met was authentic and humble, kind, and caring. What happened?

Through a relationship with Lucy McBath, a Florida mother who lost a son to gun violence and who is now a legislator, Rob began to question the marriage of the Evangelical Christian movement with the NRA and its constant promotion of unlimited access to guns. His friendship with Lucy and the questions that followed started him on a journey to questioning the conflicted ideology of a "pro-life" movement that did not seem to have any regard for the lives taken by guns. Through his learning, growth,

---

[2]Aug. 18, 2015 Tweet from @SonofBaldwin, often mistakenly attributed to James Baldwin.

[3]*The Armor of Light*, directed by Abigail Disney and Kathleen Hughes (New York: Fork Films, 2015).

[4]Rob Schenck, *Costly Grace: An Evangelical Minister's Rediscovery of Faith, Hope, and Love* (New York: Harper, 2018).

and relationships with people from different walks of life, he not only came to question unlimited access to guns, he also came to see that the ways he had fought to ban abortion had caused great harm in people's lives. Anti-abortion rhetoric and tactics dismissed the real health and livelihood of women, specifically poor women. Further, the words and actions of activists inspired violent acts and the killing of doctors who performed abortions.

When Rob came out as an Evangelical who was questioning the ideology he had been propagating for so many years, he lost everything. He lost the organization he had founded and the income he had depended on for his family. Simultaneously, he gained freedom, relationships, and clarity of conscious. He has been a role model for those who still consider themselves conservative but who seek to live their beliefs more fully with the messy nuance that comes from real life rather than the alleged purity of a rote ideology.

Rob makes a concerted effort to engage people across differences, even when people are hateful. I have seen him make the decision to *let go* of some former friends and supporters who have condemned him and to *hold on* to other relationships with people who, though they may disagree with and challenge him, continue to treat him with respect and to engage in thoughtful dialogue. Such decisions are complicated and are in frequent flux. I respect the way Rob continually reaches into his own beliefs and values to discern how to approach difficult religious and political questions. He no longer falls in line with a particular ideology for ideology's sake but holds people and their deep humanity and dignity as central in navigating the big and complex questions of life.

What About My Family?

Besides being asked about how to reach out to fundamentalists, the next most frequent question I hear is about how to navigate religious and political fault lines within family relationships. As you may imagine, this is a topic that is deeply personal to me, and I have found no easy answers. I have very different political and religious views from almost everyone in my family. At times we have handled this well, but at other times it has been horribly heartbreaking. Family can be a place where the underlying loving relationships free us to challenge assumptions and open minds and hearts to different ways of experiencing life. Family can also be a place of significant harm and pain. I think of children being rejected for being gay, or of parents and children ending their relationship simply because of how the other voted in the last election.

Last summer, I was standing on the sidelines at my son's soccer tournament when I met an amazing dad named Keith. We started talking and he shared that his son, who was fifteen years old, was at the University of Denver for the week for an intensive learning experience for students who had won a National History Day competition. His son had written a paper on the impact of Religious Freedom cases on LBGTQ people. I told him I was impressed and let him know that I was engaged in work on this issue with the Interfaith Alliance of Colorado. He went on to share how much he admired his son and how much he had learned from him. Keith was a big athletic-looking guy with light hair and big eyes. He had grown up on a farm in Iowa with three brothers and had played professional baseball. He shared that he and his wife both held many conservative views on religion and politics as well as on gender and sexuality.

Keith told me that he and his son couldn't be more different. His son knew at age fourteen that he was gay. He was an artist and a thinker and incredibly confident and smart. Keith shared that when his son first came out to him and his wife, they were not surprised, but they were challenged to rethink the views they had held previously. He shared how nervous he felt when he told his own parents and friends about his son.

I could feel Keith's authentic struggle to break through his own fear and be able to embrace his son fully, personally and publicly. The deep love Keith expressed when he talked about his son brought me to tears. I could feel how inspired he was by his son's courage, confidence, and strength. I wish every kid had a dad like Keith.

But this isn't the reality of many young people. Many know only deep pain and trauma, abuse and judgment. In cases such as these, kids are better off separating themselves from their families to protect their well-being. There are times in life when it is vital that we surround ourselves with people who love and support us regardless. Some lucky people experience that in their families, and others do not. For many people, surrounding themselves with people who love and accept them for who they are is a life-and-death issue: 67 percent of all LGBTQ young people who do not have an adult in their life who supports them will attempt suicide. That rate drops to 7 percent if they have even *one* adult in their life who supports them. For me, this statistic puts in perspective the need to assure that young people know they are loved just as they are.

For others, the situation is not life-and-death at a personal level but can be painful at the relational level. Family gatherings can feel toxic and stressful when the topics of religion or politics send people into different corners. In my own family there are some people with whom I can have a respectful and honest conversation even though we have very different religious and political views. For example, my mother and father and I can talk about what we think and why without getting defensive and angry. They continually show that they respect and support the work I do and the views I hold. I still don't understand why they vote the way they do, and they feel the same about me, but we can laugh and debate in healthy ways. With some others I have concluded that we are not able to talk about religion or politics. We know each other's views, and we know that when we try to talk about difficult issues, we each leave hurt. I regret needing to have boundaries that I feel restrict our relationship, but this is our reality.

Perhaps you have or have had a similar experience. Perhaps you, too, have to avoid engaging in heated debates with certain people. But there have probably also been times when you have had to speak up and counter someone who makes a demeaning or dehumanizing comment about someone else. You can say, "That's not my experience," and follow up by sharing your own experience that counters a hurtful or ignorant statement. Sharing out of our own heart and experience is often more helpful and more convincing than simply quoting statistics. For example, a family member challenged me about my association with the Black Lives Matter group. This family member said they believe the group is a "terrorist organization." I responded with, "That is not my experience. Ben and Amy are founders of Black Lives Matter in Denver, and they are my friends. I attended their wedding last week. We go to dinner, we work together, they watch my kids. We are friends." Through sharing personal stories with those who are creating caricatures of those they oppose, we can help humanize people and complexify assumptions.

Ultimately, we must discern from moment to moment what is most helpful for our well-being and in line with our core values. At times the relationship is too fragile and too valuable to withstand the inevitable conflict of addressing religious and political convictions. At other times we have to stand up for our core values and speak out for those experiencing marginalization or oppression, regardless of the strain it might put on family relationships.

We can also hold grace for ourselves and others and know that time and situations can change. Relationships can be healed; anger and frustration can soften. Time and space can allow room for healing and connection to occur. As we learn in the Kabbalah teachings of Gevurah and Chessed, in the law and grace of Jesus, and in yin and yang, we need both boundaries and freedom to maintain balance in our relationships and in our communities. Our task is to discern what is required in each new space and on each new day.

Questions for Reflection

1. What space of conflict have you been trying to navigate?

2. Recall a time when you had to set a clear boundary or let go of a relationship to maintain your integrity. Have you ever had to "shake the dust off your sandals"?

3. Recall a time when you have held steady in a contentious space.

4. How does your body feel when you know you are faced with your own competing values?

10

It Takes a Village: Building Community

My colleagues and I sat around a table with Congresswoman Diana DeGette and her staff. Sitting beside her were four of the "Villagers" who were formerly homeless: Cilla, Kate, Nancy, and Steve. Beside them were my fellow community leaders who helped to build this Village: Ana, Cole, and Breigh. We sat in the blazing sun at a wobbly folding table shaded by an umbrella propped in a bucket and stabilized by two bricks and rocks. We cobbled together all of the plastic chairs we could find and huddled beside the Circ House that served as a shared space. Surrounding us inside the chain-link fence decorated by the neighborhood were the eleven tiny homes in the Village that were providing space for dignity and safety. Each person has a key to their own home and is able to express their own unique personality. Just outside the fence were cranes and steelworkers building an eighteen-story condo development, one of many in the rapidly gentrifying neighborhood in north Denver.

I looked around the table at each of the people whom I had come to love, and I felt awe and gratitude. In the next breath, I began to feel nervous—hoping no one would say something that would reveal the raw and messy realities behind this moment. I hoped Cilla wouldn't pull out her new custom-designed vape pen of which she was so proud, or invite the Congresswoman into her home where, under the clutter, lay three pet snakes in small aquariums. I hoped Steve wouldn't rant about his disdain for the government or any sort of structure that holds power. Just as quickly as I had felt nervous, I felt guilty: Who am I to judge these people I love dearly and of whom I am so incredibly proud? If I am so willing to move through these spaces with grace and understanding for the complexity of life, why can't I trust others to do the same? This emotional cocktail was one that had become familiar.

***

The inner turmoil had started soon after I began working at the Interfaith Alliance of Colorado. A scrappy-looking young guy dropped in to the welcome reception being hosted for me at our local synagogue. Ben walked confidently into a room of pastors, rabbis, community leaders, and legislators, came over to me, introduced himself, and said he wanted to talk about how the faith community might support those experiencing homelessness. Grateful for his boldness and authenticity, I invited Ben to come to speak to our public policy group at the Alliance. A month later, Ben and a group of four other people carrying backpacks and "Right to Rest" t-shirts came to an Alliance meeting and shared with us statistics about homelessness and the increase in laws nationwide intended to push people into the shadows.

They shared statistics and stories of what was happening on the street—stories of people being ticketed, woken up in the night, moved from places where they were huddled seeking safety, or of police and city workers taking their belongings from them and throwing them away. They shared about a bill they wanted to introduce in the Colorado state legislature to stop this.

Although I felt compassion for them, I wasn't really sure what *we* could do for them. We gave them some tips about how to get their bill to the legislators who would need to sponsor it and asked them to come back to us when they were further along. At the prospect of our dismissing their concerns, they pleaded for our help in engaging faith leaders and communities. I was surprised they were having trouble finding support. Wouldn't this be a no-brainer for faith communities? Aren't we people of faith called to support *the poor and homeless?* Aren't faith communities one of the largest providers of charity for *the poor and homeless*? Why do they need our organizational help with this?

The more I listened and learned, the more apparent the obstacles became. Homelessness is an issue that elicits bipartisan dismissal and disdain. Although most people *want* to be supportive of, or feel pity for those living on the streets, the reality is that across the board, assumptions, fears, and stereotypes about those who are experiencing poverty and homelessness prevail. Using pejoratives for someone who "looks homeless" or "acts homeless" is still socially acceptable. Dominant cultural frameworks continue to base human value and worth on the way a person dresses, looks, and acts, what they *earn*, or what they *own*. Until I met Ben and his four colleagues, I had not really thought about the systemic realities of homelessness. I hadn't thought about how the very systems that are supposed to "help" homeless people in fact maintain oppressive power structures.

Homelessness often is the culmination of multiple forms of oppression. People of color and LGBTQ people have exponentially higher rates of homelessness compared to their percentage of the U.S. population. Women who experience domestic violence and sexual exploitation are at high risk of becoming homeless. Most appallingly, we have created or allowed laws that intentionally ensure that we are not confronted with the byproducts of decades of broken economic and social policies, policies that have resulted in a historically high number of people having insufficient resources or support to have a home, or even to survive. Laws that prevent people from sitting or lying in public spaces, from panhandling, and from covering one's self with a blanket ensure "business as usual"— that our conscience is not challenged, that we are not made uncomfortable or feel "unsafe" by the sight of a person sleeping on a sidewalk.

Through my friendships with people who have experienced homelessness, I have learned that homeless people don't cause homelessness. Broken economic and social systems mean that millions of people in our country do not have the resources necessary to survive. Simultaneously, the gap between rich and poor has increased exponentially in the past forty years. Income, wealth, and health inequality have left a few people with an obscene amount of wealth and others unable to survive. The income of the top 1 percent of Americans is forty times higher than the bottom 90 percent. The top 0.1 percent earn or have more than 198 times the income of the bottom 90 percent combined.[1] The top 1 percent of America's income earners have more than doubled their share of the nation's income since the middle of the twentieth century—the same time frame in which we have seen homelessness numbers skyrocket. It is time to recognize the vast disparity and inequality in people's daily lives.

▶ ....

(From Denver Homeless Out Loud booklet)

Homeless people don't cause homelessness. Mass homelessness has emerged as a result of federal policies and market reactions, not because of the actions of homeless people themselves.

We have not always had mass homelessness in America. In 1978, there were an estimated 100,000 people homeless in America.[2] By 2010, that number had risen to about 3.5 million people, 1.35 million of them children.[3] Before the 1980s, the last period of mass homelessness in America was during the Great Depression of the 1930s, when one million Americans were estimated to experience homelessness—a figure which pales in comparison to our current crisis. Put simply, we have vastly more people experiencing homelessness in America today than ever before.

Yet the federal response to homelessness during the Great Depression was quite different from the approaches tried in recent history. Back then, the federal government developed the New Deal, a series of safety net and social

---

[1]Elise Gould testimony before the U.S. House of Representatives Ways and Means Committee: "Decades of Rising Economic Inequality in the U.S.", available online at https://www.epi.org/publication/decades-of-rising-economic-inequality-in-the-u-s-testimony-before-the-u-s-house-of-representatives-ways-and-means-committee/ ; "The Economics of Homelessness," Wharton University of Pennsylvania Public Policy Initiative website, https://publicpolicy.wharton.upenn.edu/live/news/2594-the-economics-of-homelessness/for-students/blog/news.php.

[2]M. R. Burt, *Over the Edge: The Growth of Homelessness in the 1980s.* (New York: Russel Sage Foundation; Washington, DC: Urban Institute, 1992).

[3]E.L. Bassuk, "Ending Child Homelessness in America," *American Journal of Orthopsychiatry,* 80(4), 2010: 496–504.

welfare policies to address the shortcomings of the market. While far from perfect, New Deal policies were a successful federal response to poverty. Policies such as the federal funding of job programs, the Social Security Act, and various affordable housing programs effectively minimized the mass homelessness created during the Great Depression.

Homelessness as a widespread social ill was nearly eliminated for about four decades. Mass homelessness reemerged in America in the early 1980s, at the same time that the federal government made massive cuts to funding for affordable and low-income housing. During the 1980s, homelessness tripled or quadrupled in many US cities and, in response, emergency shelters began to open up all across America. In 1983 the Federal Emergency Management Agency (FEMA) allocated grants to fund emergency services such as food programs and overnight shelters across the country.[4]

Today, shelters have become a permanent fixture of society, with many at or exceeding capacity on most nights, while millions of people continue to struggle on the streets with no access to housing. The most recent available data shows that at least 1.3 million homeless children were enrolled in public schools during the 2013–2014 school year—nearly double the number enrolled in the 2006–2007 school year.[5]

— https://denverhomelessoutloud.files.wordpress.com/2018/01/dhol-zine_03.pdf

Even in the face of such clear disparity and inequality, we continue to refuse to fund services or housing for those who are struggling to make ends meet. I have seen the most disheartening and vile displays of humanity at neighborhood meetings and city planning and zoning sessions each time someone proposes building a shelter, low-income housing, services, or even market-rate apartments. Neighbors show up in force to yell "not in *my*

---

[4]The Emergency Food and Shelter National Board Program created by Congress on March 24, 1983. www.efsp.unitedway.org/efsp/website/index.cfm.

[5]From www2.ed.gov/policy/elsec/leg/essa/160315ehcyfactsheet072716.pdf.

backyard," repeating stereotypes, assumptions, and decades of ingrained bigotry. We, as individuals and as a country, continually fail to take any substantial action to address the crisis. Each of our faith traditions has a clear imperative that we should care for the poor and homeless.

Most such individuals or faith communities prefer to maintain their positions of power by writing checks or handing out food rather than by building real *relationships* with those living on the streets or making real material changes that will ensure that all people have access to a home and other essential resources. Confronting the bigger systemic (i.e., political) reasons for homelessness would mean challenging the status quo—the giant economic gulf that divides our communities, leaving a tragic number of people with no place to live. These are realities I have learned through showing up on the streets and meeting people experiencing homelessness.

Lest I sound too pious, I should name how difficult this learning was and continues to be for me. I live in a nice house, in a nice neighborhood, in a nice little town outside of the heart of the city. I have benefitted from and am deeply dependent on our broken economic system. My children are being raised in ways that are interwoven with this broken economic system. And yet I refuse to resign myself to the status quo. Instead, I learn, educate myself and others, take steps toward personal and political transformation, and most importantly, build *real relationships* with those who are experiencing homelessness and poverty. I learn their stories. I can work to feel solidarity in their joy and in their pain.

Doing this work is decidedly uncomfortable. Spending time on the streets is itself uncomfortable. Sometimes it is freezing, sometimes very hot. Often there is a lot of cigarette smoke, which makes my throat burn. I am frequently asked for things I cannot provide. Sometimes I am asked for things that I *could* provide, but I am not sure if I *should*. There are at times drugs on the street, or people doing drugs, something I don't typically see in my daily life. Expletives are a part of the basic street vocabulary, and stories and experiences that are shared surely challenge my worldview. Often people have had nowhere to shower, use the restroom, wash their clothes, or cut their nails. Each of these things challenges my ingrained desires for neatness and cleanliness. I consciously have to pay attention to the feelings that arise in me, notice the guilt layered in, take a breath— and let it all go in order to see the person in front of me authentically.

By no means are any of these absolutes for people who are experiencing homelessness. Many people who are experiencing homelessness are bouncing from friend to friend or sleeping in a shelter, showering, and going to work each day. More than 700,000 children (one in thirty) experience homelessness each year in the U.S.[6] All of this is difficult to see, hear, and experience, for it challenges our perceptions of ourselves, our community, and our country. Yet look and listen we must. We must educate ourselves on the realities, see ourselves as called to love and care for one another, and step into challenging spaces to *get to know people*.

By continually stepping in and allowing myself to be uncomfortable, by moving through fear, by embracing curiosity and listening, I wound up embarking on an experience that turned out to be one of the hardest and most rewarding of my life so far.

* * * *

I woke up early, rolled out of my warm bed, made my coffee, grabbed all of the extra hats, coats, and gloves I could find, and drove thirty minutes from my comfortable home to the heart of our homeless services. This is where dozens of people excluded from shelters (due to full capacity, disability, pets, or GLBTQ status) had set up tents and tarps to survive the late November chill that had set in. My new friends and partners with Denver Homeless Out Loud had asked me to show up and bear witness to what we had heard would be happening by 6:00 a.m. on that cold Tuesday morning: The city was about to "sweep" people who were living on the street, implementing the camping ban.

The *camping ban*, established five years earlier, prohibits covering oneself with a blanket or setting up a tent in a public space, and allows police to "move people along" from the places they are

---

[6]Voices of Youth Count, "Missed Opportunities: Youth Homelessness in America," https://voicesofyouthcount.org/brief/national-estimates-of-youth-homelessness/.

sleeping near the shelters. When I arrived, there were already news vans staked out waiting for the showdown.

After learning that advocates and media were waiting side by side with those experiencing homelessness, the city delayed the "sweeps." We spent hours standing on the sidewalk talking and sharing meals that had been brought by the advocacy support group Food Not Bombs. We spoke with police and city workers who were visibly uncomfortable carrying out the orders to move people along, knowing there was simply nowhere for them to go. The waiting went on for multiple days before those sleeping on the street decided to move to the City and County Building. They planned to sleep in front of the nativity display, recently placed there for the coming holidays.

At about 8 p.m., the group of about twenty people gathered all of their belongings in shopping carts and old wheelchairs and walked the ten blocks between the shelters and the City and County Building. When they finally arrived, exhausted and hungry, they set up their sleeping bags and tarps, just as they did most nights. This time they placed themselves alongside Mary, Joseph, and the baby Jesus, who were resting soundly behind a plexiglass enclosure in front of the City and County Building. At about 1 a.m., the police arrived to carry out their orders to "move people" who were lying in sleeping bags trying to stay warm in the freezing temperatures. Bundled up and shivering, I stood by to support and witness with other advocates. Most people were already huddled and sleeping when they were told to get up and move along. One man, a veteran with diabetes, peacefully resisted before the police insisted on taking his blankets as "evidence." The incident was captured on video.

As you might expect, the video went viral. This was clear evidence of the inhumane policies developed to keep people who are poor or homeless out of sight and out of mind. Denver was soon ranked as one of the worst cities for the criminalization of people experiencing homelessness, according to the National Law Center on Homelessness and Poverty.[7] Two weeks later, we received a call from the mayor's office.

---

[7] See https://nlchp.org/wp-content/uploads/2018/10/Housing-Not-Hand-cuffs.pdf .

A nation's greatness is measured by how it treats its weakest members. —Mahatma Gandhi

Baha'i
O ye rich ones on earth! The poor in your midst are My trust; guard ye My trust, and be not intent only on your own ease. —Baha'u'llah, *The Hidden Words*

Buddhism
Have compassion for all beings, rich and poor alike; each has their suffering. Some suffer too much, others too little. —Buddha

Confucianism
In a country well governed, poverty is something to be ashamed of. In a country badly governed, wealth is something to be ashamed of. —Confucius

Christianity
Then he looked up at his disciples and said: "Blessed are you who are poor, for yours is the kingdom of God. Blessed are you who are hungry now, for you will be filled. Blessed are you who weep now, for you will laugh." —Luke 6:20–21

Hinduism
He who feeds a stranger and a tired traveler with joy attains infinite religious merit. —Mahabharata XIII 7.7

Islam
And O my people! Give just measure and weight, nor withhold from the people the things that are their due: commit not evil in the land with intent to do mischief. That which is left you by Allah is best for you, if you (but) believed! —Qur'an 11:85–86

Judaism
When you reap the harvest of your land, you shall not reap to the very edges of your field, or gather the gleanings of the harvest. You shall not strip your vineyard bare, or gather the fallen grapes of your vineyard; you shall leave them for the poor and the alien: I am the Lord your God. —Leviticus 19:9–10

Sikhism
There are the lowest men among the low castes. Nanak, I shall go with them. What have I got to do with the great? God's eye of mercy falls on those who take care of the lowly. —Guru Granth Sahib, *Sri Raag*

This was the moment for which we had been waiting. We gathered at the Denver Homeless Out Loud office to make a plan. We had been building a coalition of support for a moment such as this. We had been meeting for six months with a diverse group of people. Some had experience living on the streets; others were service providers, advocates, faith leaders, foundation leaders, business owners, and neighbors. We started meeting with two clear goals: 1) to call for an end of policies that criminalize homelessness and poverty; and 2) to call for support of alternative housing such as tiny homes or other fast, affordable, and environmentally sound housing. The work that led up to this moment had been as messy as one would expect.

A broad coalition of advocates and allies means a room full of different opinions, strong personalities, various experiences of "the problem," and countless ideas for "solutions." As we worked to assure that people experiencing homelessness were at the center of the work, we realized the real obstacles to accomplish this hope. Often, people living on the streets have a hard time finding enough stability to make it to regular meetings. Usually, living on the streets brings trauma and distrust. Any of us would struggle if we never got a full night's sleep, or if we lived in a constant state of fear of our only belongings being stolen or of our bodies being violated. Although our group had high ideals, there were many times we had to settle with "good enough" organization.

Our meetings were regularly interrupted by one of my favorite people on the planet, Steve, a gruff man in his fifties who has spent most of his life on the street caring for other people and whose eyes reminded me of my great-grandfather who lived alone in the Arizona desert for more than sixty years. Steve would give the shirt off his back to someone who needed it and has high hopes and expectations of how we should all care for people unconditionally, at all times. Simultaneously, his trauma was deep, and he frequently struggled to live up to his own ideals.

Steve would regularly stand up at gatherings, curse us all out, name the vast power differences around the table, express his frustration at not being heard, and vent his general anger at the world *as it is*. He would then wait and smoke outside. After we wrapped up the meeting, several of us would step out and join Steve for our regular post-meeting "healing session" filled with apologies and expressions of love and appreciation amid frustration. In the end, it was always clear that *we were in this together*. We were each learning and growing and committed to the process.

By stepping in and showing up, I found myself falling in love— falling in love with intriguing, complicated, and love-filled people who have trauma on top of trauma. I found myself needing grace when I fall into my own privileged ways or needs for tidiness in both relationships and systems, and in my surroundings. I found myself needing to have grace for others when emotional outbursts were directed at me, or when I wasn't trusted and I couldn't figure out why. I came to appreciate the quirks and incredible gifts of each person around the table. I got to know more about people's lives and family histories, what they loved, what they hated, and *why* they were committed to building up a new world. My body warms as I recall this love and gratitude.

When we gathered to prepare for the meeting with the mayor, we knew we had to navigate interpersonal realities and power dynamics. And we were figuring out all of this on the fly. We agreed on a clear strategy, agenda, and an intentional *ask*. We thought through who should speak when and made sure Steve knew that cursing out the mayor or interspersing the expletives in his sentences like a comma would probably be counterproductive to achieving our goals.

A week later our small group of faith leaders, advocates, service providers, and people who were currently experiencing homelessness gathered outside the same City and County Building in front of which so many had slept just a few weeks before. Outside, we ran through our plan one more time, were subject to extra searches as we made our way through security, walked through the halls with marble floors and gold-framed photos of historic city leaders, went up in the elevator, and gathered in a large conference room.

Nearly a dozen people came into the room, including the sheriff, the head of health and safety, the mayor's chief of staff, and others. I suddenly felt nervous. I was being looked to as the bridge-builder in the space connecting radical activists to traditional power holders in the city government. The truth was that I had no idea what I was doing. I was reading the room, observing the human dynamics as well as the underlying power differences. I was also holding my breath and hoping no one from our party would physically threaten the mayor!

After we all sat down, the mayor walked in the room and sat down. This was the first time the mayor himself had attended a meeting with homeless advocates. We looked to Terese, from Denver Homeless Out Loud, who was set to open the meeting. Terese confidently named our hopes that the city would overturn the camping ban, and that we could receive support in changing zoning to allow for a tiny house community. Following Terese, each of the people who were currently living on the streets shared their personal stories of being scared and unable to sleep each night as they are "moved along" from one place to the next. They shared stories of what led them to realize they could not sleep in the city shelters, and of being pushed into the shadows where they are more vulnerable to becoming victims of assault and theft. Our team asked for both real support and for the city simply to clear the way for faster, easier ways for them to find a safe community. Each person spoke from the heart with clarity and confidence. I was blown away and filled with love and gratitude to be able to witness them claiming their voice and power.

In the end, the mayor would not budge on the camping ban, though he did give an order that blankets no longer be confiscated as evidence. After further conversation, the mayor asked the city staff to help "get to yes" on being able to allow a tiny house village despite the current zoning obstacles. We walked out cheering, proud that we had both held it together and followed our plan, and grateful to have made progress in gaining support for the vision of building a tiny house village for people experiencing homelessness. Now, the hard work would begin.

Building a Village

At the time, we thought the hard part would be navigating zoning codes and raising money. We brought in more leaders, specifically Nathan and Cole, who wound up becoming two of my close friends and resilient and persistent leaders. They met weekly with city leadership, learned how to read the city's legal documents, and tapped into their idealistic hopes to build community in ways that embodied our values rooted in mutual relationships. Together we pushed through obstacles that felt hopeless, such as realizing just hours before we had to submit them that we needed a general contractor to sign off on our architectural drawings. We welcomed little miracles as they came—in the form of a general contractor who was by chance meeting one room over and who boldly jumped into our project, and a new charitable foundation which was looking to fund just such an operation.

The chaos of each moment cannot be contained in neat sentences on the clean pages of a book. Each and every day we wondered whether we would go down in flames while we sought to stay focused on the task at hand: build a village and move people from the street into homes and community. Some of our personal relationships became bogged down by broken trust or outbursts of violence. We ached to overcome the centuries of division in racism and classism that are carried in our bones. We watched as villagers struggled with depression and addiction, which tend to rear their heads when people have the repetitive trauma of instability and fear. Our hearts were broken when we had leaders from the streets understandably decide they needed to move on, leaving us with a vacuum where we had been grateful to have stability.

Simultaneously, holiness and feelings of sincere gratitude that can only come when we are working for something bigger than ourselves would wash over me in moments of exhaustion, frustration, and joy. Sometimes I would look around and feel completely overwhelmed by what was happening. I knew we were building the world we imagined and doing the real work that must be done if we are ever to see collective liberation. During one meeting we were locked out of the space in which we had planned to meet, so I pulled a blanket out of my car along with a snack bucket I keep in the car for the kids. We had our meeting on the ground on a busy street corner, and no one thought twice about it. We sat cross-legged eating fruit snacks and granola bars, wondering how we would get the money to move to the next step. After vigorous debate, we all agreed that we would keep moving forward and trust that the money would follow. And it did.

Eventually, we had all of the zoning, permits, and funding, and were able to work together with Denver Homeless Out Loud to find people ready for homes and to build a tiny house village together. Led by volunteers from our local Mennonite Disaster Service, over the three-month period more than three hundred people came to build homes or to provide food and connect with the community. In the end, we had eleven homes ready. Nathan led the community in a healing service to let go of the weight of the struggle and pain that had been picked up along the way. Terese began the work of building covenants with the community who would create shared governance agreements. Cole continued the work of navigating city relationships, raising money, and holding all of the pieces together. And we had a big celebration, invited all of the neighbors, ate pizza, danced, and laughed together at how far we had come.

Building Houses Is Easy, Building Community Is Hard

After the houses were built and the residents had moved in, the real work began. There is a reason our societal instincts are first to push people into the shadows or even to spend millions on mass apartments and expect people to find their own way. Living *with* other people is difficult—especially when people are carrying the pain and trauma that so often accompanies life on the streets. At the same time, our most deep-seated human needs lie in a sense of belonging and a connection to one another. Central to our goals with the Village was to build a model that established personal and communal connection and dignity and to break out of the "service provider" and "service recipient" power structures.

However, these power structures are both woven into our personal and relational memory and far more efficient and orderly. To challenge systems of oppression, we all had to learn how to find new paths forward, and to get comfortable with a bit of chaos. Three years later, we are still figuring it out. We have all learned and grown and navigated conflict and a shocking number of unexpected obstacles. More than anything, we realize that weaving people back together—*loving people*—is both the most important and the hardest thing when working in the muck of social change.

At every step of the way, we had to tap into our roots to remember our core values, which for many of us were found in the teachings of our faith traditions. We had to be conscious of our context and the more significant social and political structures at play. We were not only experiencing the consequences of decades of broken policy and economic and social inequality, we were also in a local political environment with a booming city that was quickly developing a reputation for toxic gentrification and mass homelessness. We were working to keep marginalized people at the center while consciously building credibility with traditional power structures to get city leaders to provide the support we needed.

We were facing our own fears each day, fears of both external factors such as neighbors, zoning, and fundraising, and internal factors such as power battles, violent outbursts, and mental health crises. We tried to stay curious as we continually learned how to build a model that is both aligned with our values and sustainable for the long haul. And through it all, we developed a real love for one another. The love we fostered helped carry us through the difficult days and was seen clearly when we were covered by the news or visited by congresspeople.

* * * *

Congresswoman Diana DeGette had learned about our project and wanted to see firsthand the excellent work happening in her district. Although the Villagers had grown accustomed to news cameras, volunteer groups, and even drop-in visitors coming to "watch them in their homes," a visit from a congresswoman felt like a big deal. Cilla and Kate had both prepared their homes to share with the group. They were proud, even though I was slightly nervous (remember the snakes?). When the day came, and the congresswoman and her delegation stood up from the wobbly table, I watched Cilla, Kate, Nancy, and Steve talk to the congresswoman and her team as if they were old friends. I was overwhelmed to see them each glow with pride as they told her about their jobs and school and the ways in which the Village has helped them find safety and stability and healing.

And then they started walking toward Cilla's house, where three snakes would be there to greet them. I held my breath waiting for the moment this beautiful and significant moment would all fall apart into chaos. As Cilla opened her door for the congresswoman, she shared with pride that her snakes Coco, Mocha, and Peanut were just inside. Congresswoman DeGette lovingly took a step back, expressed appreciation for the pet snakes and kindly stood in the doorway, peeking her head in before telling Cilla how beautiful her home was and giving her a big hug. As I watched the interactions and the genuine connections happening between the Villagers, our team of support, and the staff from the congresswoman's office, I realized how often I don't give people enough credit. We are all just people navigating this chaotic world in the best ways we can. Daily we are each seeking to love one another *in the midst of it all.*

> *Charity* is the act of giving money, food, or other kinds of help to people who are poor or sick.
>
> *Justice* is the quality of being just; righteousness, equitableness, or moral rightness: to uphold the justice of a cause.
>
> The difference: Charity is goodwill without a transition of power; justice is moving toward equity and righteousness through the sharing of power.

Questions for Reflection

1. When have you experienced a "mutual relationship" across difference? What does this mean to you?

2. When have you been challenged to let go of your assumptions about another person?

3. Is it easier to write a check or to build a relationship with someone in need of support? Why?

4. Do you have any big dreams of ways you might work with others to address a need in your community? What would be required to make that happen?

Conclusion: In It for the Long Haul

I awoke in a fog. My bones ached with exhaustion. I felt heavy and didn't want to move. Tears streamed down my face, and I wasn't entirely sure why. I made my way out to my patio, curled myself up in a chair with a blanket, and stared silently out at the newly blooming trees in my yard. I picked up my phone and texted my coworker Nathan and shared with him something I had never shared before. I was depressed, and I needed a day to rest. I had experienced depression before, but never like this. My friend and coworker immediately gave me love and told me that he would take care of things at the office, that our team had it covered, that I did not need to carry the world. More tears streamed down my cheeks, this time tears of gratitude and humility.

I am used to being the one to *give* words of grace and compassion; I am not great at *receiving* them. In our organization, we have built a culture of holistic care to honor the fullness of our humanity, which includes stepping back when we need rest and asking for help when we need support. However, at that moment I realized that I still believed that I should "pull myself up by my bootstraps" and get on with the day. On this morning, the tapes that played in my head were words of shame and doubt. As much as I tried, I couldn't pull myself up. I had no choice but to receive the kindness and support that Nathan was offering.

So, I stopped. I stopped working and caring for others. I stopped thinking of my next big idea and building my to-do list. I eventually made my way to the trail near my house, where I went for a slow walk to feel the sun on my face and the ground under my feet. While walking, I saw on the trail ahead of me Karen, the matriarch of our neighborhood. She asked how I was, and I was honest: I was tired and overwhelmed by the demands of mothering and working and loving. She responded with compassion and walked with me to the owl's nest down the way. For a long while, we stood and watched the great horned owl perch and guard his babies growing in the giant nest one tree over. I learned all about the long history of owls in the neighborhood and how owls don't build new nests but reuse hawks' nests from the last season. We eventually said goodbye, and I kept slow-walking until I came across a blue heron in a pond on the side of the trail. I sat on the ground and quietly watched as she gracefully lifted her long legs to move through the marsh on the bottom of the water before diving her head into the water and coming up with a fish.

Eventually, I made my way back home and curled up on the couch for a nap. I called my mom, who knew by my voice that I was not myself and offered me gentle words of support. My husband came home early from work and held me, and together we went for another slow walk. It took a good week for the fog to lift. And in that time, my loved ones, coworkers, husband, parents, neighbors, and friends caught me. And I let them.

This loving one another is hard work. The drama and pain of the world can feel intensely overwhelming, especially when we're deep in the weeds of policy, community organizing, and advocacy work. It is easy to begin to feel isolated and to develop a myopic vision of our lives and of this time in which we are living. When the fog lifted, I remembered that I was not alone. To think we are in this alone is to have bought into a toxic culture of individualism. To get trapped in the frustration and longing of wanting to see our immediate progress is to fall into our cultural desire for instant gratification. Rather than becoming trapped in guilt over these real feelings, we are better to notice them, take a breath, and let them go. The alternative option of becoming absorbed by the paralysis of guilt is a primary tool of maintaining oppression and division. Succumbing to the rat-race frenzy of killing ourselves for the sake of social change feeds division, resentment, and dysfunction.

We become whole when we remember that we are in this together. My well-being is connected to yours, *for better or worse*. Our sacred texts are filled with story after story of people striving to survive and struggling to overcome the violence, division, and fear that is woven into our lives. We walk in a centuries-long line of people who have ached for a life of freedom and opportunity for themselves and their children. We walk in a centuries-long line of people who sang songs, danced, and cooked delicious meals, even when life was hard. We walk in a centuries-long line of resilient people who have worked each day to love one another in the best way they know how.

This image brings me joy. There has been no historical time when all was *right*. There are moments in which we briefly feel that all is right, but those moments are always fleeting. The story of our humanity is a long story of seeking to find connections and thriving in the midst of separation, struggle, and suffering. Although this may seem depressing to some, it brings me feelings of solidarity, peace, and resilience.

Life Is Chaotic. Life Is Holy.

The work of engaging in religion and politics is the work of showing up with love each and every day and asking, "What does love look like here?" I have come to believe that love is all about finding *peace* in the midst of the chaos, finding *connections* in the midst of division, experiencing *healing* between the breaths of exhaustion and suffering, and working for ways of *loving*— personally and systemically—in the midst of the overwhelming fear, anger, and division that swirls around us. When we commit to this work, this way of being and moving through the world, we might find moments of deep joy, even euphoric gratitude. It is toward this that the mystics of our various religions call us.

When I am bogged down by the birth pangs of trying to care for others in the midst of so much division, I remember that evolution takes time and is uncomfortable, even painful. Just as the mama seal who snapped at the wandering baby seal reminded me that day in La Jolla, we are wired to protect ourselves and our own. Breaking through these instincts to genuinely love and care for the well-being and thriving of *all* people is a long, painful, and necessarily intentional process. We are going where few people have gone before. And yet there are centuries of people who have come before us who have left us legacies of resilience, have created connection in the midst of division, have spoken up for what is right, and have put their bodies in the places needed to move our communities toward justice.

When I feel trapped in that fog, and when I take the time to let myself be cared for, I think of the cloud of witnesses who have modeled how to move through the most critical and most challenging spaces of life with courage and resilience. I think about the Israelites wandering in the wilderness for forty years. Forty years! An entire generation is feeling lost, hungry, frustrated, and impatient. I think of Harriet Tubman, patiently and fiercely taking beatings and threats to her life to keep moving people out of slavery one by one for decades and decades. Even after being struck in the head and having her skull fractured, and after having a bounty placed on her life, she kept moving forward and fighting for real freedom for herself and others. I think of Ella Baker fighting Jim Crow, first as a secretary, then as an organizer, and finally as a director of movements and organizations. She plugged away each day, often behind the scenes, to build and fight fearlessly for justice. I think of the seventy years it took for women to earn the right to vote in the United States. Today it is hard to remember that for centuries half of our human population was deemed incapable of thinking clearly enough to discern their own future. I think of each of the people throughout our history who have loved and imagined and worked each day to further real *justice for all*.

Some years ago, I heard some words that have stayed with me: "Everyone wants to be a part of the revolution, but nobody wants to do the dishes." I imagine all those revolutionary people scrubbing the pans, and filling glasses of water, and shopping for snacks, and locking up the doors after a long night. I imagine back porches and coffee shops, circles of people sitting together laughing, crying, sharing stories, and commiserating about the frustrating setbacks. I imagine people checking in on one another and lifting one another up when they couldn't stand on their own. I imagine friends getting word that someone they love is sick and needs help, and I imagine them dropping their work and going to help the ones in need. I wonder about Harriet Tubman's friends: Who prodded her to sit down and take a break? Who rubbed Ella Baker's feet when she was tired, or held her close when she wasn't sure she could go any further? Who were the women who met together and plotted and planned in living rooms and kitchens, building the case for suffrage?

We need one another. Across all of our differences, across all of the hot topics that tear us apart, we need to support one another through the difficult tasks of standing in contentious spaces, rooting ourselves in what is right, and fearlessly showing up and taking action to build just communities. I guess this is why I feel so sad when people won't talk about "religion" and "politics." Religion and politics are about life and how we live together. Is what we watched last on Netflix, or the weather that is on its way, more important than we are? Don't get me wrong: I, too, talk about my favorite Netflix shows, and I certainly complain about the weather (especially when it is cold). But we must dare to dig a little deeper. We must not forget to think and reflect, to ask the more profound questions, to challenge our assumptions, and to get curious about all of the layers. We must intentionally see the face of God in one another and wonder what each person teaches us about the creator of it all. Inevitably we will mess up. We all do. That's human. We will cause one another pain, and we will feel the pain of another's actions. How will we deal with it? Where will we draw lines? Where will we share grace? How will we show up for one another again and again?

These are the questions that stir me as I move into chaotic spaces to bring people together across our religious differences. These are the questions I sit with when working with advocates to build a strategy for advancing legislation that will expand rights for all. These are the questions that I mull as I pick up my kids from school and get to know parents on the soccer sidelines. This is living. It is both holy *and* chaotic.

* * * *

I was standing at the starting line ready to cheer on my daughters at the state cross country meet when I received a news alert on my phone that there was an active shooter at a synagogue in Pittsburg. My heart plummeted. I sent a text to our Interfaith Alliance of Colorado team to give love and support and to ask them to watch events so we would know how best to respond. I texted each of my rabbi friends to let them know I was thinking of them and knew how painful this must be. I took a breath, put my phone in my pocket, and cheered on my daughters.

After the race had finished and I had hugged and congratulated my daughters, I found a quiet place and called my friend Scott, who leads the Anti-Defamation League. By this time, we knew that eleven people had been killed and seven injured. We knew that this had been a brazen act of anti-Semitism and that the perpetrator had explicitly stated the synagogue's support for refugees as a motive for his hate and violence. We began planning a vigil to bring our community in Denver together right away.

The next night we gathered at Temple Emanuel, where the governor, the mayor, all of our state legislators, as well as senators and congressional representatives, sat side by side with more than two thousand people from all walks of life who filed into the sanctuary. Once the sanctuary was full, an overflow room filled with one thousand more people. Friends from the Sikh community offered to bring water and chai tea to those who were grieving. They worked in the back kitchen, where my husband joined them to try to increase the amount of tea they were making as people kept coming.

After everyone was seated, I walked in with government officials, rabbis, and leaders from the interfaith community who gathered on the *bimah,* or stage, at the front of the sanctuary. It happened that I was the only woman at the front. We went up one by one and offered our words of support and compassion. I recall almost everyone talking about the need for people to come together at this time. When it was my time to speak, I stepped to the podium and looked out at the overwhelming crowd of three thousand people who were unified in their grief and their longing for a different way forward.

I spoke from the heart, prompted by words I had jotted down on a piece of scratch paper that afternoon. I shared words of heartbreak and solidarity, and I placed the event in the context of the attacks on black churches that had happened the same week and the centuries of antisemitism that are both symptoms of the diseases that divide us and make us ignorant of our connections to one another. I then said that we must call on our leaders to unite us and not divide us, and we must vote (it was a week before the 2018 election). At that, the crowd jumped to their feet and clapped with a standing ovation. I was taken aback by their reaction. I did not think I had said anything revolutionary. Perhaps it was because I was the only woman on stage, or because of the emotion of the moment, but my words evoked strong reactions from the crowd. I learned later that a few people had walked out after I spoke. That night I received a few scathing emails as well as countless moving messages thanking me for my words and energy that night.

After I had rested and had time to catch my breath, I sat down to read my emails, both the positive and the negative. Out of the four angry emails I received, one was from an Orthodox rabbi who hadn't actually been at the event but had heard that some of his congregants had been angered by what I had said. His email was full of anger and sadness, and I felt it necessary to reach out. In consultation with Scott from the Anti-Defamation League, I responded. I first offered my sympathy for the pain their community was experiencing at that time, and then apologized that some people had been hurt by my words. I sent a copy of the words I had actually spoken and shared that my hope was simply to name that we must come together in this time when so much seeks to tear us apart. I offered to meet him for coffee to get to know each other better and for further conversation.

He responded with an apology for the angry tone of his email. He said that he had been sad to miss the vigil. He was feeling guilty for not being with his congregants that night and said that perhaps he had taken that out on me in his email. He took me up on my offer to meet, and we set a time. Two weeks later, we met at a local coffee shop and found a quiet place. I apologized again that my words had felt divisive for people in their community and expressed my real intention that we seek ways to understand one another better. He responded by sharing that the root of the problem was in the divisions *within* the Jewish community. He named that the tension between more politically conservative and more politically liberal Jewish people was being felt in his community. Not only were his people feeling continued disagreement on how to address the Israel and Palestine conflict, they were also feeling vastly different emotions about President Trump.

The rabbi went on to share that his son lives in a settlement in Hebron, and he fears daily for his son's life. He shared that the security of Israel means more to him than anything else, and that this security is deeply personal. I shared that I understood the pain of political divides in families. I told him about how most of my family supported Trump, and that I feel sadness about the ways we are not able to talk about or agree on political issues that shape our lives.

As we each shared our heartbreak about the ways in which we feel the vast political divisions of our time, it was as if a common space opened between us. The energy between us lightened and his face softened. He started telling me about his grandkids, and I shared about my children. He told me that his dog had died the previous week and he was struggling to go through the days without her by his side. I said that I had never felt a pain more significant than the pain of losing a dog, and then we both pulled out our phones and shared pictures of our beloved pets.

Before the conversation ended, we came back around to the topic of the Israel/Palestine conflict. I shared that one of my close friends is Palestinian and that I had traveled to Israel in 2009. I told him that my relationships with rabbis and Palestinian friends had left me feeling conflicted and heartbroken by both the occupation and the clear and lasting anti-Semitism that permeates our conversations about the conflict. He offered to send me some reading, which I gladly accepted. We both gave thanks for the time we had shared and offered to continue the conversation at any time, knowing we came from very different places.

* * * *

I walked away with a deep sense that our most significant connection was our shared heartbreak. We each feel the sadness and pain that comes when we have lost our connection to one another. Mutual liberation, personally and politically, is found in the *holy and chaotic* spaces of weaving ourselves back together, one day at a time, in radical, practical ways. As we keep moving forward, as generations of people have before us, I hope that we will not avoid *religion and politics*. I hope that we will take time to think, learn, and open ourselves to the critical questions before us, and step into the conversation with determination and resilience. I hope that we will embark on these holy and chaotic topics with a commitment to the long-haul revolutionary work of loving one another and building a world where all can thrive.

The arc of the moral universe is long, but it bends toward justice.
—Martin Luther King, Jr.

Nothing that is worth doing can be achieved in our lifetime; therefore we must be saved by hope. Nothing which is true or beautiful or good makes complete sense in any immediate context of history; therefore we must be saved by faith. Nothing we do, however virtuous, can be accomplished alone; therefore we are saved by love. No virtuous act is quite as virtuous from the standpoint of our friend or foe as it is from our standpoint. Therefore we must be saved by the final form of love which is forgiveness.
—Reinhold Niebuhr

We have not even to risk the adventure alone, for the heroes of all time have gone before us—the labyrinth is thoroughly known. We have only to follow the thread of the heropath, and Where we had thought to find an abomination, we shall find a god; where we had thought to slay another, we shall slay ourselves; where we had thought to travel outward, we shall come to the center of our own existence. And where we had thought to be alone, we shall be with all the world.
—Joseph Campbell

Where, after all, do universal human rights begin? In small places, close to home...Such are the places where every man, woman, and child seeks equal justice, equal opportunity, equal dignity without discrimination.
—Eleanor Roosevelt

Acknowledgments

I am forever grateful to those who support, shape, and muddle through life with me. Thank you to all who are mentioned in the stories I share in these pages; I hope I have captured my experiences in ways that honor you. Thanks to my parents, Steve and Jerrie, for making me who I am—and loving me even though our views of the world differ. You have helped me to be able to navigate complexity rooted in love and compassion. Thank you to my sister Jill and her husband TJ, to Craig and Margaret, Jim, Cheryl, Clint, Brandie, and to all of my nieces and nephews. Thank you to my lifelong friends, Annette, Katie, and Ande. Our families are the ground for learning to connect, care, and love one another in the midst of our many differences.

Thank you to the communities who helped me learn that life doesn't have to be perfect to stick together. To all of the amazing neighbors we have had over the years who have been friends and partners in creating community. To Heart of the Rockies Christian Church, Jeff and Janet, Scott and Becca, and the many people who "grew me" in those years. Thanks to Brite Divinity School, to Valerie Forstman, Steve Sprinkle, Joretta Marshall, Warren Carter, Keri Day, and Namsoon Kang. Thanks to Ridglea Christian Church, the Multi-Cultural Alliance, Beth and Rob, and to all who loved our family in our home-away-from-home in Fort Worth. Thanks to the folks at South Broadway whom I loved dearly. And thanks to First Plymouth and Eric Smith, who caught us and have provided a place of stability through lots of change. Thanks to our Disciples community, to Chalice Press, Brad, and Deb, and the editors who helped clarify my words.

Thank you to all of you at the Interfaith Alliance of Colorado who have let me fly and who taught me how to be fully *me-in-*

community. Thank you to Jim Ryan, Dilpreet Jammu, Tom Wolfe, Nathan Woodliff Stanley, Brian Henderson, Hal Simmons, Brandon Peterson, Jill Wildenberg, and Iman Jodeh. Thank you to Terese, Steal, Ray, Cilla, Jerry, Ben, Kayvan, PJ, Vern, and Luna. Thank you to Ismail and Ismail, and Harold and Claudia, and Angela. Thank you to Dawn Riley Duval and Tawana Davis for your incredible patience and real friendship. Thank you to Nathan Davis Hunt for catching me, and for being a partner in this work of imagining and moving through the muck. Thank you to Jane for your may years of helping me slow down and feel my center.

Thank you to Alissa Rausch for processing each piece of our messy lives and the stories on these pages as we run miles and miles on the highline canal. I can imagine no better friend than you.

Most of all, thank you to Kyle, my partner in life. We have each been many different people over these years, and I am so grateful our orbits continue to rotate together. I love negotiating love and marriage, parenting, education, work, and our human revolution, together.

And finally, thank you to Mia, Faith, and Ryan for giving me the best role ever as your mom, and for putting up with me learning on the job. You are everything to me: My favorite moments are when we are all in the kitchen with music blasting, and are laughing, dancing, wrestling, eating, and playing. You make life pure joy.

30 Stories from 8 Faith Traditions

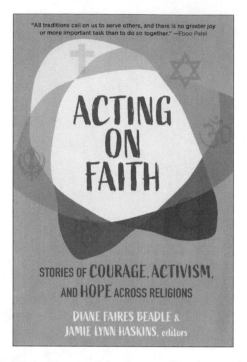

"All traditions call on us to serve others, and there is no greater joy or more important task than to do so together." —Eboo Patel

ACTING ON FAITH

STORIES OF COURAGE, ACTIVISM, AND HOPE ACROSS RELIGIONS

DIANE FAIRES BEADLE &
JAMIE LYNN HASKINS, editors

Different faiths, shared hopes. Are we more alike than we know? In these first-person stories from diverse voices of faith, learn how our different religious beliefs inspire courageous acts of justice and love amid the world's violence and divisions. *Acting on Faith* cultivates hope in our common values and encourages personal action through concrete examples of faithfulness, justice, and love from those on the front lines of activism and advocacy. Reflection questions make *Acting on Faith* perfect for small group study or a private devotional.

ISBN 9780827200890

chalice press
You Want to Change the World. So Do We.

ChalicePress.com • 800-366-3383

We need a better way of relating
to one another and responding to
controversial issues—
a way that transcends political partisanship and
emphasizes universal care, mutual concern, and the
flourishing of the common good.

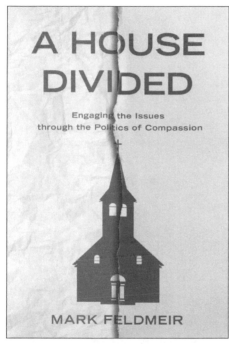

A HOUSE
DIVIDED

Engaging the Issues
through the Politics of Compassion

MARK FELDMEIR

ISBN 9780827200968

A House Divided examines
eight of the most divisive
issues of our day—
climate change, racism,
immigration, healthcare,
medical aid in dying, Islamic
extremism, homosexuality,
and social isolation and
suicide—through the lens of
a politics of love, seeking to
identify those shared values
that affirm our commonality
and inspire a more creative
and collaborative approach
to finding practical
solutions and healing our
divisions.

Each chapter includes a
study guide for small group
conversations.

"If every parent of every child reads this book, this next generation will truly create the kind of world we all want to live in."
– Kerry Connelly, author of *Good White Racist? Confronting Your Role in Racial Injustice*

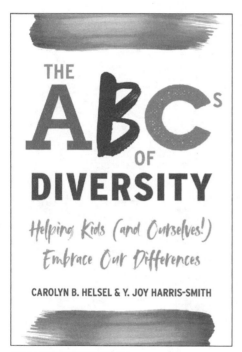

ISBN 9780827200937

Teach the language of difference with *The ABCs of Diversity*.

How do we raise the next generation to respect and learn from people who look or believe differently than they do? From two educators who are also moms comes a guide to help parents and other teachers navigate conversations about all kinds of diversity. This practical resource includes activities to build compassion and empathy among differing religions, classes, races, genders, abilities, political affiliations, sexual orientations, nationalities, and more.

chalice press
You Want to Change the World. So Do We.

ChalicePress.com • 800-366-3383